Gerrymandering

Gerrymandering

The Politics of Redistricting in the United States

Stephen K. Medvic

polity

First published in 2021 by Polity Press

Polity Press
65 Bridge Street
Cambridge CB2 1UR, UK

Polity Press
101 Station Landing
Suite 300
Medford, MA 02155, USA

ISBN-13: 978-1-5095-3686-3
ISBN-13: 978-1-5095-3687-0 (pb)

A catalogue record for this book is available from the British Library.

Library of Congress Cataloging-in-Publication Data
Names: Medvic, Stephen K, author.
Title: Gerrymandering : the politics of redistricting in the United States
   / Stephen K Medvic.
Description: Medford : Polity Press, 2021. | Includes bibliographical
   references and index. | Summary: "A rigorous exposé of the practice of
   gerrymandering and its impact on American democracy"-- Provided by
   publisher.
Identifiers: LCCN 2020046421 (print) | LCCN 2020046422 (ebook) | ISBN
   9781509536863 (Hardback) | ISBN 9781509536870 (Paperback) | ISBN
   9781509536887 (ePub)
Subjects: LCSH: Gerrymandering--United States. | Politics,
   Practical--United States.
Classification: LCC JK1341 .M44 2021 (print) | LCC JK1341 (ebook) | DDC
   328.73/073455--dc23
LC record available at https://lccn.loc.gov/2020046421
LC ebook record available at https://lccn.loc.gov/2020046422

Typeset in 11 on 14 pt Sabon by
Servis Filmsetting Ltd, Stockport, Cheshire
Printed and bound in Great Britain by Short Run Press

For further information on Polity, visit our website: politybooks.com

Contents

Figures and Tables

Acknowledgements

Writing this book was made significantly more pleasurable because of the professionalism and good humor of the entire Polity team. I thank Louise Knight for her support of the project and for her patience when I fell behind schedule (which, sadly, happened more than once). I had the good fortune to work with three outstanding editorial assistants: Nekane Tanaka Galdos, Sophie Wright, and, especially, Inès Boxman, who was on board for most of the time I was writing. Her periodic check-ins served as gentle, but effective, nudges to keep my nose to the grindstone. The production process, overseen by Neil de Cort, was efficient and, from my perspective at least, seamless. Ian Tuttle did a fantastic job of copy-editing the manuscript and saved me from more than one embarrassing mistake.

I owe the greatest debt of gratitude to my wife, Laura. As I worked on this book, I was constantly inspired by the grace with which she handles her work as Registrar of Franklin & Marshall College, the graduate classes she's taking, and all the other responsibilities she has on her plate. Her energy is infectious and I can't imagine facing life's challenges without her love and encouragement.

CHAPTER I

What's the Problem?

In the 2012 US elections, a majority of voters who went to the polls in Pennsylvania cast a ballot for the Democratic candidate for Congress in their district. Yet, of the 18 seats from Pennsylvania in the US House of Representatives, the Republican Party won 13 of them. In other words, though they garnered a bit more than 50 percent of the congressional vote, Democrats won only a little over 25 percent of the seats. In four other states that year, the party that won a majority of the votes in congressional races got fewer than half the seats.[1] In North Carolina in 2016, Republican House candidates received 53 percent of the vote but 10 of 13, or 77 percent, of North Carolina's House seats.[2] How can these results have happened? Perhaps more importantly, is there any way in which these outcomes can be considered democratic?

This book addresses both of those questions. The short answer to the first of them is that the congressional district boundaries in Pennsylvania, like legislative district lines in many states, were gerrymandered. Gerrymandering is the process of drawing legislative district boundaries to give one party (or group of voters) an electoral advantage over others.

Gerrymandering in the United States is quite unpopular with the public. According to a bipartisan poll conducted in December 2018, 63 percent of all likely 2020 presidential voters had an unfavorable view of partisan gerrymandering. Another 32 percent had no opinion while just 5 percent had a favorable view.[3] Those views were shared, with only slight variation in the percentages, by Democrats, Independents, and Republicans alike. When respondents were asked if they would prefer districts with no partisan bias, even if it meant fewer seats for their own party, or districts with partisan bias, assuming that their own party would win more seats, only 15 percent chose biased districts while 65 percent preferred unbiased districts.[4]

Nevertheless, when legislators have the opportunity to gerrymander district lines, many – perhaps most – of them will seize the opportunity. Voters are unlikely to punish their own party for doing so (despite their stated preference for unbiased districts) and legislators can enhance their party's power by creating additional districts in which they have an electoral edge. With little downside and the potential for gaining seats in the state legislature or in Congress, gerrymandering is hard for politicians to resist.

The second of our questions is the more difficult one. How one answers it will depend on what one means by 'democracy' and whether one thinks the redistricting process should be a normal part of politics. Though democratic elections are expected to be free and fair, it's not immediately clear what would constitute a violation of this expectation.

The rest of this chapter will introduce gerrymandering by explaining, in a bit more detail, what it is and why it occurs. Gerrymandering is not unique to the United States but its practice here is in many ways exceptional. The chapter will then address the reasons that gerrymandering stirs so much controversy. Beyond the obvious power struggle that gerrymandering initiates, there are competing visions of how democracy ought to operate that are at play.

The Need to Draw District Boundaries

In any political system with meaningful legislative elections that take place in districts not demarcated by otherwise permanent boundaries (e.g., state or national boundaries), the lines around legislative districts will have to be drawn. In most places, these lines will be redrawn periodically to account for population shifts. This process of redrawing district lines is called redistricting or boundary delimitation.[5]

In the United States, redistricting typically takes place every ten years, following the constitutionally mandated national census. For congressional representation, census data is used for reapportionment, or the process of adjusting the number of members of the House of Representatives from each state based on changes in population. For example, as a result of the 2010 Census, Texas gained four seats in the House while New York and Ohio each lost two.[6] District lines in states that gain or lose seats will obviously have to be redrawn. However, they'll also be redrawn, even if only slightly, in states that did not gain or lose seats.[7] That's because, as we'll see later in the book, it is now a legal requirement that legislative districts within a state have equal population sizes. This applies to state legislative districts as well, so census data will be used to redraw state House and Senate districts to ensure equal population sizes in those districts.

The states are responsible for drawing state legislative and congressional district boundaries. In most states, the state legislature draws district lines and adopts the new maps as they would any normal piece of legislation. Some states, however, let commissions established for this purpose draw the lines for state legislative and/or congressional districts. Regardless of the model a state employs, the process is virtually always political.

These two facts – that district boundaries must be redrawn regularly and that the redistricting process is political – create opportunities for those who wish to gerrymander districts. In countries where districts correspond to pre-existing administrative units, there is no opportunity to gerrymander because there is no need to redraw district boundaries. In Israel, for example, all 120 members of the Knesset (the national legislature) are elected nationally by proportional representation. In other words, the national border serves as the district boundary for the one (nationwide) legislative district. Few countries that do not redraw district lines are that extreme. There are a number in which electoral districts correspond to predetermined sub-national governmental jurisdictions (e.g., provinces or states).[8] In the remaining countries, where districts don't correspond to permanent territorial units, gerrymandering becomes a possibility.

Even in countries that utilize redistricting commissions, gerrymandering can occur. Of course, the extent to which this is possible depends on how the commission is constructed and how it operates. Nevertheless, even in places where redistricting commissions are supposed to be neutral, forms of gerrymandering can take place. The United Kingdom, for example, uses Boundary Commissions (one each for England, Scotland, Wales, and Northern Ireland) to establish parliamentary constituencies. Despite the fact that the Commissions are designed to be independent and non-partisan, Ron Johnston, Charles Pattie, and David Rossiter have found significant bias (in favor of the Labour Party) in the results of UK general elections through 2005. In part, this bias was the result of "increased efficiency of Labour's votes."[9] This increased efficiency of the vote, in turn, is explained (at least in part) by the Labour Party's efforts to influence boundaries during the Public Inquiries conducted by the Commissions.[10] Thus, even when partisan operatives don't control the redistricting process, they may nonetheless influence it.

It should be noted that electoral systems using single-member legislative districts (i.e., one representative per district) almost inevitably produce disproportional results. The percentage of seats won by the victorious party will usually be larger than the percentage of votes they received because of the winner-take-all nature of these districts. Winning districts with 75, 60, or even 51 percent of the vote results in 100 percent of the representation for those districts.[11] However, this disproportionality is not the same as bias, as Johnston and his colleagues point out.[12] We'll discuss various definitions, and measures, of partisan bias later in the book. For now, it's worth noting that gerrymandering, by definition, results in biased electoral results and bias is the chief problem with gerrymandering.

Of course, gerrymandering can sometimes be used for purposes other than maximizing the number of seats for a party. The protection of incumbents is another, quite common, use of gerrymandering (sometimes referred to as "bipartisan gerrymandering"). Though it is possible to protect incumbents while also maximizing seats for a party, it is generally thought to be difficult to do both effectively. To protect an incumbent in one place often means giving up a seat to the other party elsewhere. Regardless of why it's being done, however, the root problem with gerrymandering is the same – it creates an unlevel playing field in a given district.

The need to redraw district lines, in and of itself, doesn't create biased maps.[13] Indeed, unbiased districts can be drawn, as the experience of many countries, and even many American states, demonstrates. Instead, it's the political nature of the redistricting process that makes gerrymandering so hard to avoid.

To say that the redistricting process is political is not to imply that it is corrupt.[14] It is simply to recognize that politically motivated actors will use any legal means to achieve their goals.[15] To a non-partisan observer, this may appear ethically problematic or, at the very least, distasteful as it seems to place narrow self-interest above the common good. The partisan, however, sees their goals as synonymous with the greater good. If they are inclined to consider the ethical implications of their actions, they are likely to find those actions perfectly acceptable. They are, after all, pursuing the greater good (as conceived from their partisan perspective).

Put another way, the politics of redistricting simply reflect the underlying tensions within a given political system. As political scientists Bernard Grofman and Lisa Handley so wisely note in the introduction to their collection of comparative studies of the subject,

> Redistricting can be thought of as politics in a microcosm. Redistricting struggles are fought on several levels in ways that reflect both the politics of ideas and the politics of naked power. The allocation of seats and the drawing of constituency boundaries have practical, legal, and philosophical implications. To reflect on redistricting forces us to think about the underlying bases of political representation and the related fundamental issues of democratic theory.[16]

It is to the philosophical implications that we now turn our attention. It is easy to condemn gerrymandering as a perversion of democratic processes. However, doing so requires a clear understanding of what it means to say a process is 'democratic.' As we'll see, that is more complicated than it might first appear.

Fair Elections

It is commonplace to hear that democratic elections must be "free and fair." But what, exactly, does that mean? Drawing on

Robert Dahl's classic work, Jørgen Elklit and Palle Svensson argue that elections must avoid coercion if they are to be free.[17] Voters must be allowed to fully participate in the process, meaning their rights to assemble peaceably, speak freely, and associate expressively, among others, must be protected. Free elections, according to Elklit and Svensson, entail "the right and the opportunity to choose one thing over another."[18]

Whereas free elections must avoid coercion, fair elections must ensure impartiality. Fairness "involves both *regularity* (the unbiased application of rules) and *reasonableness* (the not-too-unequal distribution of relevant resources among competitors)."[19] That is, election rules must apply equally to everyone, and all political parties and candidates must have roughly equal access to resources that are necessary to be competitive. Equality, then, is a vital aspect of electoral fairness. It is the basis, for instance, of the "one person, one vote" standard.

Free elections occur almost automatically in free countries. It's nearly impossible to imagine a country with protections for free speech or a free media somehow curtailing those freedoms in the electoral arena. Fairness, on the other hand, requires the conscious development and application of impartial electoral rules. A country may be judged to be fair, in general, according to any number of standards and still have election laws that fail to ensure electoral fairness.

We might think of electoral fairness, following the political theorist Dennis Thompson, as "electoral justice." Electoral justice, in turn, "is a species of procedural justice. It seeks fair terms of cooperation, a set of practices that all citizens could accept as an equitable basis for making collective decisions."[20] Importantly, Thompson argues that we must judge electoral processes independently of the outcome of any given election (or set of elections). In other words, we can't decide that an electoral rule is fair or just simply because we're happy with the result of an election. We have to assess electoral rules and procedures in and of themselves. For Thompson, electoral rules "are just to the extent that they realize principles that could be freely adopted under conditions of equal power. In the case of electoral justice, the principles express the values of equal respect, free choice, and popular sovereignty."[21]

Thompson readily acknowledges that people will interpret these principles differently. What sorts of (and how many) alternatives must voters be given if their choices are to be free? How equal must voters, or candidates, be in order to achieve an equal level of respect and what is required to ensure such equality? Must the electoral system always enable the majority to win if "the people" are to rule? Of course, the problem is not only that it isn't obvious what kinds of procedural arrangements are necessary to achieve equality, liberty, and popular sovereignty. It's that these principles can sometimes come into conflict with one another. The freedom of a billionaire to spend as much as they'd like supporting the party or candidate of their choice conflicts with the ability of citizens to have equal voice in the process or of candidates to have roughly equal resources for contesting an election.

It is unlikely, therefore, that debates over electoral rules and procedures – including redistricting and gerrymandering – will take the form of a democratic side versus an undemocratic side. Instead, the debate is over competing visions of democracy. Thus, the most productive way to frame the debate over gerrymandering is as follows: One side believes redistricting should be considered part of the regular legislative or, more generally, political process, while the other side believes that redistricting should be thought of as a periodic adjustment to the foundational rules of the political system. The former will necessarily be 'political' and partisan; the latter aims to be apolitical and non-partisan.

As it happens, most of those who embrace the political/partisan perspective, or what I'll call the "realpolitik redistricting" argument, are political practitioners such as campaign consultants and party operatives. There are some scholars in this camp but most of its adherents work in the realm of practical politics. The other side of the debate, which we might call the "civic redistricting" argument, consists mostly of legal scholars, political scientists, and reform activists. Thus, in a given sphere – "real world" politics or academia – the debate may be lopsided. Taken as a whole, however, there are as many advocates of one perspective as there are of the other. These advocates simply come from different worlds and are, undoubtedly, influenced by their experiences in those different domains.

The realpolitik redistricting argument rests on the assumption that no process involving political actors can be apolitical, nor can the product of such a process be neutral. Even if some such processes could be apolitical, redistricting is not likely to be one of them. As the political scientist Justin Buchler explains, given the winner-take-all nature of legislative districts in the United States, the procedures for drawing district boundaries will inevitably determine winners and losers, broadly defined, in those districts. Indeed, according to Buchler, choices about redistricting rules are "*indistinguishable* from the question of who should win and who should lose."[22] This holds both for the choice of actors responsible for redistricting and for the specific decision-making rules those actors choose to utilize to draw maps. "Thus," writes Buchler, "there can be no apolitical redistricting in any meaningful sense of the term because the choice of delegation is as 'political' as the choice of algorithm."[23]

In partisan and bi-partisan (or incumbent protection) gerrymanders, it is easier to see how the process picks winners and losers. However, even if district lines are drawn to enhance competition between the parties (an approach Buchler calls a "competitive gerrymander"[24]), winners and losers are being determined. If competitive districts make it more likely that a centrist candidate will win, then centrist voters are the winners, and non-centrists are losers. If, given voter and candidate polarization, a non-centrist is sure to win, then non-centrists on the winning candidate's side of the spectrum are the winners and centrists and non-centrists on the other side of the spectrum are the losers.[25]

Critical to the realpolitik argument is the claim that voters aren't powerless in the process. They know that redistricting takes place in the year following the census and they can vote for candidates who will draw lines the way they'd prefer them to be drawn. As the political commentator Kevin Williamson puts it,

> If Democrats are unhappy with Republican domination of the state legislatures and governorships – and they should be unhappy – then they have a much more direct option [than going to court]: They can go into the states and ask people for their votes in legislative races and in gubernatorial elections. If they find that route difficult, then maybe the Democrats should be rethinking what they're trying to sell people.[26]

According to this view, when the voters put one party in charge of the entire post-census legislative process, they are likely to be satisfied with the legislative maps that party draws. (If, on the other hand, voters produce divided government – that is, control of at least one chamber in the state legislature is in the hands of one party while the governor is a member of the other party – then they apparently prefer compromise in the redistricting process.)

In fact, the realpolitik perspective maintains that it is undemocratic to take redistricting out of the democratic process. "Redistricting is not politicized. It is political," writes

Williamson. "For the Democrats and the Supreme Court to try to step in and take away from the state legislatures their long-standing right to draw up legislative districts as they see fit is much more deeply undemocratic than anything Republican gerrymanderers ever dreamt up."[27] Take, for instance, the use of independent redistricting commissions to draw district boundaries. Members of such a commission, like judges, may appear non-partisan but they undoubtedly have partisan loyalties. It's not realistic to expect that people involved in public affairs will be apolitical. But even if they were non-partisan, redistricting commissions with the power to unilaterally determine district lines would not be accountable to the voters. What recourse would voters have if a redistricting commission produced district maps the voters found objectionable?

Finally, this perspective maintains that the rules of the game were established at the founding of the country, when the Constitution was adopted. Those rules – essentially, the Constitution – can be amended, but that process itself is provided for in the Constitution. However, in the absence of an attempt to change the Constitution, formally or informally as part of what might be referred to as "constitutional politics," "normal politics" reigns.[28] Normal politics is the familiar, day-to-day struggle over "who gets what, when, and how," as the political scientist Harold Lasswell famously put it.[29] Redistricting, then, is simply part of normal politics.

One might argue, of course, that the Constitution forbids partisan gerrymandering. We will consider that argument in a later chapter. For now, suffice it to say that the realpolitik viewpoint does not believe partisan gerrymandering is constitutionally prohibited. To understand why, it's worth quoting law professors Larry Alexander and Saikrishna Prakash at length:

> There is no natural or obviously correct way of dividing voters into equipopulous districts. People have diverse preferences about how that ought to occur. Nor are there obviously wrong or improper ways of allocating voters across equipopulous districts. If we are to believe that the Constitution mandates certain districting and electioneering ideals, then we have to suppose that the Constitution implicitly imposes certain rather controversial and complex preferences on the conduct of districting and elections. Necessarily, we have to imagine that the Constitution also implicitly rejects all other plausible preferences about districting and elections. We think that such claims have no merit.[30]

The countervailing viewpoint, the civic redistricting perspective, acknowledges that neutrality in human processes is difficult to achieve. Nonetheless, it takes the position that we should strive to find a set of rules governing the operation of elections that both parties (or, indeed, all parties) can accept. Without opening a Pandora's box of contemporary political theory, this position is grounded in the notion of public reason and the claim that political actors ought to be reasonable in their public deliberations.[31] To be reasonable, a person must be willing "to live by rules that can be justified to similarly motivated citizens on grounds that they could accept."[32] There is, then, an important element of reciprocity at work here. What is fair for one side ought to be fair for the other (or others). We'll find a version of reciprocity later in the book in the concept of partisan symmetry.

With respect to processes governing democratic elections, reasonable people would likely agree that the purpose should be to establish robust competition. Competitive elections are, after all, a hallmark of democracy. In a series of academic papers, the legal scholars Samuel Issacharoff and Richard Pildes develop a framework for adjudicating electoral rules that seeks to maintain "competitive partisan political environments that avoid insider lockups of democratic politics."[33] Whereas current jurisprudence interprets election law in the context of individual rights and state interests, Issacharoff and Pildes argue that the focus should be on "the background rules that structure partisan political competition."[34] "The key to our argument," they write,

> is to view appropriate democratic politics as akin in important respects to a robustly competitive market – a market whose vitality depends on both clear rules of engagement and on the ritual cleansing born of competition. Only through an appropriately competitive partisan environment can one of the central goals of democratic politics be realized: that the policy outcomes of the political process be responsive to the interests and views of citizens. But politics shares with all markets a vulnerability to anticompetitive behavior. In political markets, anticompetitive entities alter the rules of engagement to protect established powers from the risk of successful challenge.[35]

Gerrymandering, of course, is the quintessential anticompetitive tactic. Drawing on the theory of political competition, Issacharoff finds problematic even a legislative map that is mutually agreed upon by both parties if that map gives the parties a distinct electoral advantage in their respective districts. This, he argues, causes voters harm based on the "constriction of the competitive process by which voters can express choice."[36] Issacharoff analogizes the collusive behavior of these parties to companies, say Coke and Pepsi, that agree to sell their products in different geographical regions to avoid competing with one another. Such an agreement would be illegal on antitrust grounds. Partisan cartels, he maintains, should be treated similarly.[37]

What of the argument made by the realpolitik redistricting camp that voters will decide who they want drawing district boundaries? The response from the civic redistricting perspective is that such a claim is naïve in several respects. First of all, voters are faced with the relevant choice just once or twice every ten years, in elections immediately preceding the census count (i.e., election years ending in "8" and/or "0," depending on when the officials responsible for redistricting will be elected). This decennial opportunity doesn't really allow voters to influence the redistricting process. The exigencies of a given election year – is it a presidential or a midterm election year; is the economy strong or weak – are likely to have more impact on voters' choices than is the fact that the redistricting cycle starts in the near future. Furthermore, even if voters wanted to cast their ballots solely on the basis of their redistricting preferences, they have no way of assessing potential maps because those can't be drawn until the census has taken place. As a result, voters are left with only one option, namely, the crude partisan determination that their party should control the redistricting process. However, as the polls cited at the beginning of this chapter suggest, the majority of voters do not want gerrymandered districts, even if such districts are biased in their party's favor. A victorious party that believes it has a mandate to run the redistricting process is almost certainly mistaken. Finally, in elections for legislators who will be involved in the upcoming redistricting cycle, district boundaries drawn in the previous round of redistricting will constrain voters' choices. If those boundaries were the result of partisan gerrymandering, the choices in the current pre-redistricting elections will already have been unduly influenced.

Many of those who would like to see politics removed from the redistricting process believe that the best way to do so is to take responsibility for drawing district lines away from elected officials. Opponents argue that it is more democratic to allow elected officials, who are accountable to the electorate, to draw district maps rather than unelected redistricting commissions or judges, who don't have to answer to anyone for their work.

However, those who take the civic redistricting position believe both that elected officials are not as accountable for the maps they draw as we might think and that redistricting commissions can be designed to ensure accountability.

Imagine what would be required of voters if they were to hold accountable the elected officials drawing maps. A voter would have to be aware of the range of potential maps being considered during the redistricting process and would have to develop a preference for one of the maps (per legislative chamber). Not many voters are apt to gather this information, or even have access to it, and few would come to a judgment on it. If, by some chance, most voters did identify their preferred maps, they could only then punish those responsible for supporting district lines they object to *after* the maps had been drawn. Thus, even if they were to defeat the offending mapmakers at the next election, the maps those officials drew would be in use for the rest of the decade. (Some states do allow mid-decade redistricting, though in practice this rarely happens and its legality in most of those states is ambiguous at this point.[38]) Furthermore, the whole point of gerrymandering is to shield one party, or a group of incumbents, from serious electoral threat. How likely is it, then, that elected officials in newly gerrymandered districts are going to be vulnerable in the next election? To the extent that elected officials are invulnerable, there is no real mechanism for accountability.

We'll discuss redistricting commissions in detail later in the book. For now, it should simply be noted that there are ways to design independent redistricting commissions so that they are accountable to the citizenry. Indeed, there are ways to design these commissions to allow the public at least some role in the process.[39] Accountability can be preserved even if district lines aren't drawn by elected officials.

Those who take the civic redistricting perspective insist that redistricting is not – and shouldn't be – part of normal politics. It is not part of normal politics because it is not concerned with the identification of policy problems and solutions. And it should not be part of normal politics because it lays the foundation for normal politics by delineating the playing field. To the extent that politics plays a role in the redistricting process, the normal politics that occur after lines have been drawn will be skewed. That means, in part, that normal politics may not reflect the underlying preferences of the electorate.

Of course, the redistricting process is not part of constitutional politics either. To be sure, there is a debate over whether partisan gerrymandering is permitted by the Constitution (with most of those in the civic redistricting camp believing it is not, for reasons that will be discussed elsewhere in this book). Those engaged in that debate are, no doubt, involved in constitutional politics. But the redistricting process itself isn't part of any attempt to alter our understanding of our most foundational document.[40] Redistricting, then, occurs – or should occur – within a unique space in American politics. Without reaching the lofty arena of constitutional politics, it ought to nonetheless remain above normal politics.

In the end, these competing perspectives on the nature of redistricting differ not in terms of how democratic they are but in terms of the way they conceive of democracy. One takes the view that democracy is conflictual and is shot through with politics. This view of democracy is like the American humorist Finley Peter Dunne's view of politics – it "ain't beanbag."[41] A free society allows individuals, typically acting in groups, to pursue their own self-interest. This makes democracy a battle between groups of people over the future direction of the country. Given the stakes, we should expect those groups to play hardball and any legal means to achieve one's ends are permitted.

The other view is that democracy is about achieving the common good. From this perspective, too much partisanship is antithetical to that purpose. While there will be vigorous debate over what the common good requires, the pursuit of one's own conception of the common good does not justify bending the basic rules of the game. If the only constraint on political actors' behavior is what is legally permissible, the norms of democracy – including the expectation of fair play – will erode and deep divisions will emerge in society. Under those conditions, the common good is nearly impossible to achieve.

Representation

Another important consideration in the gerrymandering debate is the nature of representation. Ultimately, a representative democracy must translate the desires of the public into policy. Exactly how that is to be done isn't obvious.

The theoretical literature on representation is vast and it is beyond the scope of this chapter to even begin to summarize it.[42] For our purposes, representation will refer to the relationship between elected officials and their constituents in which elected officials act on behalf of their constituents in matters of governing. Though representation is always descriptive to some extent (i.e., reflecting demographic characteristics like race, religion, and gender), most of the current discussion about representation in the context of redistricting concerns substantive representation, or the representation of constituents' policy preferences and ideological perspectives.[43] The assumption is that constituents' preferences ought to be reflected in the voting records of their representatives. If, for example, most constituents in a given area prefer conservative policies, their representatives should support conservative policies.

Perhaps the most obvious way of thinking about representation is to consider whether individual legislators are
representative of their constituents. This is commonly referred
as "dyadic representation," because it compares one representative to one constituency.[44] Many would argue that ideological
and/or partisan agreement between the representative and
his or her constituents is of paramount importance. Indeed,
from this perspective, maximizing such agreement ought to be
the goal of those who draw district lines. In districts that are
gerrymandered to be safe for one party, most voters will share
that party affiliation and are likely to be satisfied with their
representation.[45] One might object that representatives from
such districts are less likely to be responsive to the voters or
are less likely to be held accountable by them. The response to
such an objection is that accountability is maintained through
primary elections.

From another perspective, the creation of safe districts
amounts to rigging the system. A common refrain from this
side of the debate is that when gerrymandering is allowed to
occur, politicians are picking their voters before voters can pick
their politicians. From this point of view, then, the goal is competitive elections. District lines should be drawn in such a way
as to maximize competition in as many districts as possible.[46]
Of course, given that only one representative will be elected
per district, a competitive district in which preferences are split
roughly 50-50 will mean that about half the constituency will
always be unhappy with its representation. Be that as it may,
competitive elections are thought to be more effective in holding incumbents accountable, giving voters a meaningful choice
over their representation, and generating more excitement and,
consequently, more participation than uncompetitive elections.
These effects, it is argued, are vital for a healthy democracy.

An alternative to dyadic representation is "collective representation." In this formulation, what matters is whether legislators, taken as a whole, accurately reflect the aggregate policy preferences of the public.[47] If a majority in a given state wants to increase the minimum wage but the legislative majority opposes such an increase, the public would lack collective representation on this issue.[48]

There are those who would argue that the question of whether an institution, like Congress, is representative in a collective sense is largely irrelevant. The American system of government, they argue, is not designed to achieve collective representation at least in majoritarian terms. Features like the separation of powers, bicameralism, and federalism mean that it is purposefully difficult to translate majority preferences into policy. Representation in institutions like the US Senate and the presidency (via the Electoral College) is geographically based, which can easily distort policy preferences. In the House of Representatives, single-member districts with plurality winners mean that the relationship between the seats a party wins and the votes it receives will be distorted, even without conscious gerrymandering.[49] Thus, perfect correspondence between the policy preferences of the public as a whole and of the legislators collectively (let alone the policy output of the legislature) is, by design, nearly impossible to achieve.

Others believe a significant level of collective representation is necessary if the people are to rule in any meaningful way. Legislatures should produce policies that the electorate desires. When they don't, they are not providing the responsiveness that democracy requires. There are many reasons why the public's policy preferences might not be reflected in actual public policy. The many "veto players" in the American system (e.g., the president, majorities in the House and in the Senate, and filibuster-wielding minority in the Senate) are a key reason for the disconnect. But another is that the partisan makeup of the legislature might not match the partisan preferences of the electorate (partisanship being a shorthand indicator of a set of policy preferences). For those who believe collective representation is indispensable for democracy, disproportionate election outcomes, like those mentioned at the outset of this chapter, are *prima facie* evidence that election processes are undemocratic. And while disproportionate outcomes are always possible in a system of single-member plurality elections, they are made more likely by partisan gerrymandering.

It is, of course, possible for individual representatives to do a good job representing the views of most of their constituents (dyadic representation) while the legislature as a whole does not represent the views of the public very well in the aggregate (collective representation). The reverse may also be true. Tables 1.1 and 1.2 offer hypothetical illustrations of how representa-

Table 1.1 Hypothetical Example of Good Dyadic (District-Level) Representation but Poor Collective Representation			
District	Conservatives	Liberals	Moderates
1	63 √	37	0
2	71 √	29	0
3	65 √	32	3
4	74 √	22	4
5	67 √	30	3
6	65 √	35	0
7	63 √	35	2
8	76 √	20	4
9	65 √	35	0
10	70 √	25	0
Average support	67.9%	30%	1.6%
Seats	100% (10)	0% (0)	0% (0)

Note: Numbers in the last three columns indicate the percentage of the district that holds a given ideological point of view. Check marks indicate the point of view held by the district's representative.

Table 1.2 Hypothetical Example of Poor Dyadic (District-Level) Representation but Good Collective Representation

District	Conservatives	Liberals	Moderates
1	49 √	48	3
2	48	49 √	3
3	49 √	48	3
4	48	49 √	3
5	49 √	48	3
6	48	49 √	3
7	49 √	48	3
8	48	49 √	3
9	49 √	48	3
10	48	49 √	3
Average support	48.5%	48.5%	3%
Seats	50% (5)	50% (5)	0% (0)

Note: Numbers in the last three columns indicate the percentage of the district that holds a given ideological point of view. Check marks indicate the point of view held by the district's representative.

tion can go awry. In table 1.1, a clear majority in each district share conservative views with the representative from the district. This is good dyadic representation.

Collectively, however, the population is not well represented as nearly a third of the electorate is liberal and yet not a single representative holds liberal views. In table 1.2, the opposite problem exists. Collective representation is very good as the even split between conservative and liberal representatives (five each) mirrors the breakdown of conservatives and liberals in the population (48.5 percent of the population in each category). District-level representation is not particularly good, however, because the representative from each district represents a view that commands less than a majority.

As contrived as these hypotheticals may seem, results like these do exist. In Connecticut, following the 2018 midterm elections, Republicans held none of the five seats in the US House of Representative even though they received 38 percent of the vote statewide (as in table 1.1). Similarly, Democrats won 35 percent of the House vote in Arkansas but took none of the state's four seats. A real-world example of table 1.2 is harder to find but the results of Minnesota's congressional elections in 2018 are close. In five of the eight House districts, the winner garnered less than 56 percent of the vote leaving a very large portion of the electorate (roughly 44 to 49 percent) presumably unhappy with its representation. Statewide, however, the division of seats (five Democratic and three Republican) is reasonably close to the statewide division of votes (55 percent Democratic and 44 percent Republican).

Regardless of their real-world applicability, the hypotheticals serve to illustrate the fact that dyadic and collective representation do not necessarily occur simultaneously. They can, of course, but even the most neutral district boundaries will not automatically produce robust levels of both types of representation. Importantly for our purposes, these hypotheticals also test the priorities of the two sides of the redistricting debate. If forced to choose one of these two scenarios as the most preferable, those in the realpolitik camp are more likely to prefer table 1.1 to table 1.2 while those who favor civic redistricting would likely prefer table 1.2 to table 1.1.

The realpolitik view accepts the partisan nature of the process and is likely to also view district-level representation as a critical element in the delicate balance established by the framers of the Constitution. As such, those in this camp are far more likely to be satisfied with solid dyadic representation based on partisan or ideological preferences. Those who wish to take partisanship out of the redistricting process prefer districts to be drawn in ways that will enhance accountability and responsiveness to the entire population, not just a primary

electorate. To the extent that the public's partisan preferences should influence representation, they should be reflected
proportionally in the number of seats each party receives statewide.[50] After all, it's the people *as a whole* who should govern.

At this point, a word about incumbents is probably in order.
Much of the previous discussion has concerned partisan gerrymandering. That is, the debate is about whether parties should
be allowed to draw district boundaries that benefit only their
candidates. However, bipartisan gerrymandering – or incumbent protection gerrymandering – is also controversial. The
realpolitik camp is likely to see nothing wrong with protecting
incumbents because, ultimately, incumbent protection is still
partisan. In order to create districts that are safe for existing
incumbents of both parties, the partisanship of districts has to
be taken into account. This, from the realpolitik point of view,
does not preclude the possibility that incumbents will be held
accountable and could be kicked out of office. It's simply that
the primary electorate, or voters within the incumbent's party,
are the ones who hold the incumbent accountable.

It is precisely because incumbent protection is nonetheless
partisan that the advocates of civic redistricting oppose it as
well. To be sure, some of the opposition from this perspective
is motivated by an anti-incumbent attitude. The fear is that
incumbents in safe districts are not likely to be challenged by
another candidate from their own party in large part because
the party organization will discourage it. Even if incumbents
were to receive primary challenges, voters in their party are
unlikely to turn them out because name recognition has such
a powerful impact on the vote. Thus, safe incumbents can
stay in office for as long as they want, increasing the possibility that they will become out of touch with their constituents.
Ultimately, however, those in the civic redistricting camp dislike bipartisan gerrymandering for the same reason they dislike

partisan gerrymandering, namely, that in any given district, it stacks the deck in favor of one party over the other.

Plan of the Book

In the chapters that follow, we will examine gerrymandering in far greater detail. Chapter 2 traces the development and evolution of gerrymandering over time. Gerrymandering dates to the early nineteenth century, though there are examples to be found in the American Colonial period. Initially, legislative districts were coterminous with city, town, or county boundaries. However, politicians eventually realized that they could create electoral districts for partisan advantage by combining jurisdictions in whole or in part. Prior to the 'reapportionment revolution' of the 1960s, which will be discussed in detail in chapter 3, legislative districts were not required to have an equal number of people in them. Malapportionment meant that rural areas had far more representation than urban areas but also that the drawing of district lines could be done relatively haphazardly. In addition, those drawing district lines before the 1960s did not have access to computers for use in the process. Thus, after the 1960s, when districts had to contain an equal number of people and, eventually, when technology could be employed to identify voters at the household level, gerrymandering became far more precise.

Chapter 3 reviews the fate of gerrymandering in the courts. It begins by describing the 'reapportionment revolution' of the 1960s, which prohibited malapportionment of legislative districts and established the principle of "one-person, one-vote," or equality of representation. To realize this ideal, legislative districts within states must contain equal populations (or as close to equal as possible). In the years following the reapportionment revolution, the courts and Congress turned attention to the potential for gerrymandered districts to dilute the votes of racial minorities and/or partisans. The creation of 'majority-minority' districts was an attempt to address the former but often reduced partisan competition in the process. The most recent legal battles over gerrymandering concern partisan bias in district maps. These battles, as we'll see, have been won by those defending the practice of partisan gerrymandering.

Chapter 4 begins by providing a more detailed account of the normal redistricting process. It then describes how partisan majorities gerrymander districts for electoral advantage. They do this either by placing as many supporters of the other party as possible into a minimal number of districts, thereby concentrating their voting strength ('packing') or by spreading supporters of the other party throughout many districts, thereby diluting their voting power ('cracking'). The chapter will illustrate these tactics with hypothetical and real-world examples. It will also discuss the use of computer technology in the redistricting/gerrymandering process.

The consequences of redistricting and gerrymandering will be explored in chapter 5. The primary focus will be on the effect of redistricting on candidates and parties, including its influence on the level of competition, partisan advantage, and the incumbency advantage. Redistricting may also affect voters directly, so the chapter considers its impact on voter turnout and vote choice. Finally, gerrymandering is often blamed for increasing levels of polarization. The chapter concludes with a look at the evidence with respect to this claim. In many of these areas, the scholarly research comes to contradictory conclusions and, in general, the results are mixed in terms of whether gerrymandering has significant consequences on elections.

The final chapter of the book will begin with a review of the normative arguments for and against gerrymandering and will make a case for reform of the process. It will then consider several ideas for reforming the redistricting process to eliminate, or constrain, gerrymandering. The most prominent idea is the use of redistricting commissions. Such commissions, which draft district boundaries and are populated by persons who may or may not be elected officials, vary in their independence from legislators. The most radical reform proposal to be considered is the use of multimember districts with proportional election rules. Moving to such an electoral system would greatly reduce the need for redistricting and would more fairly represent the partisan preferences of the electorate.

Conclusion

Redistricting – and gerrymandering specifically – can be exasperating, but it is also a fascinating aspect of American politics. As long as there are electoral districts that don't correspond to permanent boundaries, district lines will have to be drawn. How, exactly, to do that will inevitably generate debate.

The debate over the redistricting process is not a debate over democratic versus undemocratic procedures. It is a debate between competing visions of how democracy should operate. Is democracy inherently conflictual, with various groups in society struggling to protect their interests through any legal means necessary, or is it potentially conciliatory, with an identifiable common good that can be achieved if neutral rules for politics are in place? One perspective on redistricting – the realpolitik view – is rooted in the former while another – civic redistricting – is based on the latter.

This chapter considered the role of redistricting in realizing two fundamental elements of modern democracy – fair elections and effective representation. What, exactly, is required for elections to be considered fair and what standard are we to use to judge the effectiveness of representation? Should redistricting be considered part of "normal politics" or must it be part of a pre-political process establishing the rules within which normal politics will take place? Should we seek the effective representation of individual districts or of the entire population of a state or the nation (and which should we prioritize if we cannot have both)?

The answers to those questions are complicated. The aim of this chapter has been to explore that complexity and to suggest that applying one set of principles to the redistricting process will likely mean sacrificing another set of principles. Regardless of one's feelings about gerrymandering, the hope is that this chapter will have made readers aware of the validity of competing perspectives on the practice.

CHAPTER 2

A Brief History of Gerrymandering

If we were to establish a representative assembly today, for our state or for the country as a whole, how might we do it? Specifically, how would representation work? Where would representatives come from and whom (or what) would they represent? To the modern citizen, it might seem obvious that *people* are represented and, on top of that, they are to be represented *equally*. That has not always been the case in representative assemblies in the United States.

This chapter traces the development and evolution of American electoral districts over time. It begins by examining "corporate" representation in colonial assemblies and the boundary manipulation of towns and counties that sometimes occurred during the colonial period. Following independence from Great Britain, states began to base representation on population and many opted to elect representatives from single-member districts. As a result, the drawing of district boundaries became an increasingly vital political activity in the early American republic, as did gerrymandering.

By the middle of the nineteenth century, fierce party competition and a requirement that states hold congressional elections in single-member districts (with some exceptions) meant that the ability to draw district boundaries had become extremely valuable. It was also a frequent activity, as many states redrew district lines multiple times per decade. Interestingly, the opposite occurred in the early twentieth century as states often refused to redistrict in response to population growth in urban areas.

The history of drawing district boundaries in the United States is, in many ways, a history of gerrymandering. The manipulation of districts has taken a number of forms, but the purpose has always been the same, namely, to gain political advantage in elections. That gerrymandering has such a long history in the United States suggests that, without legal limitations, it is virtually inevitable.

Districts in Early American History

There were representative assemblies in America long before Congress and, indeed, well before there were state legislatures. Colonial assemblies contained councilors appointed by the Crown or by the colony's proprietors but they quickly incorporated elected members as well. As Peverill Squire notes in his study of the evolution of American legislatures, colonial assemblies "emerged at different times and for different reasons" but they all "rapidly evolved into representative bodies as it became geographically impracticable for all freemen to participate in their regular (and often frequent) sessions."[1] Interestingly, the divergent viewpoints of appointed magistrates and elected delegates eventually led to the earliest bicameral assemblies in America (i.e., one chamber for the magistrates and one for the delegates).[2]

Elected representation in colonial assemblies, and the state legislatures that emerged from them, was based on geography. That is, towns and counties, not people, were represented in assemblies. The theory underlying this system of territorial, or "corporate," representation was that the members of a local community would naturally share attitudes and interest. As Rosemarie Zagarri put it in her study of representation in early American history, "Each geographic unit was thought to be an organic, cohesive community, whose residents knew one another, held common values, and shared compatible economic interests."[3] Thus, the interests of communities, and not of individuals, were paramount and deserved representation in the assembly.

Initially, geographical units were given equal representation. For instance, the Virginia General Assembly, established in 1619, consisted of "two Burgesses from each Plantation [or settlement] freely . . . elected by the inhabitants thereof."[4] Fairly early in the colonial experience, however, some allowance was made for greater representation for towns with significantly larger populations. Thus, while the Plymouth Colony allowed each town to elect two freemen, it granted the town of Plymouth four representatives.[5] Georgia's original assembly allowed every "village, town, or district having ten families settled within its limits" to elect one representative; "those having thirty families" could "depute two persons;" and Savannah was given four representatives.[6] And in Virginia, representation for each settlement would vary from one to six delegates within ten years of the first meeting of the House of Burgesses.[7]

Since towns or counties were the basis for representation, one would assume that boundary lines were essentially permanent, having been established when a given town or county was created. However, as Elmer Griffith explains in his classic study of gerrymandering,

> At the present time the boundaries of counties are rarely modified. But in the colonial period necessity required that they be frequently adjusted. This custom of changing county lines was frequently abused and was made a means of securing political advantage, precisely as in after years district boundaries were changed and altered for the same reason.[8]

To be sure, the political advantage sought by manipulating town and county boundaries was not partisan as we would use the term today. Instead, the division was between "the prerogative and measures of the governor and those of the people; in other words, between the representative of the crown and the democratic branch of the government."[9] Nevertheless, this political manipulation of boundaries indicates just how early the urge to gerrymander appeared in American politics.

Griffith claims that the earliest case of gerrymandering occurred in the colony of Pennsylvania in the first few years of the eighteenth century.[10] However, close examination of the political struggles between the counties surrounding Philadelphia and the city itself reveals that the power-enhancing method used by the counties was, first, apportionment and, later, suffrage restrictions. While the counties Bucks, Chester, and Philadelphia (excluding the city) were originally given four representatives in the assembly, the city was given just two. Later, when county representation was increased to eight, representation for the city remained unchanged. As the population in the city grew, suffrage requirements were set at "possession of fifty pounds in personal property or a free holding, neither of which was easy to secure."[11] As the population in the western part of the colony grew, the representatives from the three eastern counties made sure to "erect new counties slowly, if at all, and to restrict their representation in the Assembly."[12] None of this is gerrymandering, *per se*, unless you consider the separation of the city from any nearby county, or the unwillingness to establish new counties, as a decision about where to draw lines. Still, Griffith maintains that Pennsylvania had "dissimilar election districts which were continued for partisan political purposes," and that these "artificial and heterogeneous" districts were established "to the interest of one class of citizens and against a rival portion."[13]

Another of Griffith's early examples of gerrymandering, the colony of North Carolina, is far more compelling as a case of boundary manipulation. "As early as the year 1732," writes Griffith, "the governor was engaged in dividing precincts for his own political ends."[14] To achieve those ends, the governor and his councilors might turn a single existing precinct into as many as ten new precincts; some of the altered precincts contained as few as thirty families. The goal of all such activity, which garnered "serious objection" at the time, was to produce a lower house (ostensibly of the people) that was in agreement with the magistrates' upper house.[15]

Once the American colonies declared independence from Great Britain, state legislatures were formed to replace colonial assemblies (with provincial congresses operating in the interim[16]). "In a very concrete way," writes Squire, "the colonial assemblies morphed into the first state legislatures."[17] This was particularly true for lower chambers in bicameral legislatures, which existed in all but two states, since those chambers were already built upon republican principles of representation.[18] Thus, the common practice of allocating representation according to existing political units, like towns and counties, continued in most states.

Nevertheless, some states took the opportunity independence afforded, with its attendant spirit of equality, to experiment with representation based on population. This alternative to corporate (i.e., territorial) representation was referred to as "proportional representation."[19] According to this system, a ratio of representatives to people would be established (e.g., one representative per 100 citizens) and applied to districts throughout the state. Interestingly, Zagarri found that the size of the state influenced a state's decision about the basis of representation. "[T]he legislators in smaller states," she notes, "concluded that the traditional system, based on territory, was adequate for their needs, whereas the legislators in larger states believed that a newer method, based on population, should be adopted."[20]

Though not recognized widely, if at all, at the time, representation based on population meant that drawing district boundaries would become a critical process in the makeup of state legislatures. As Zagarri notes, "Districts could be drawn to encompass a certain number of people – and the boundaries redrawn as the population increased or decreased."[21] It also meant, of course, that district boundaries could more easily be manipulated for political gain.

The design of the upper chambers in state legislatures had to change in one key way from those in their colonial forerunners. Because representatives in upper chambers had been appointed in the colonial assemblies, provisions for electing members to the upper chamber had to be established.[22] In some states, members of the upper house would be selected by members of the lower house. In most, however, the people elected their state senators.

State senate districts typically corresponded to existing counties. Griffith notes that four states – Massachusetts, New Hampshire, New York, and Virginia – "established artificial senatorial districts."[23] In two of those states, however, districts were comprised of "very simple and necessary groupings" that either combined a limited number of counties into one district or split counties into separate districts.[24] In New York, the state was divided into just four senatorial districts but each district consisted of a combination of counties.[25] As a result, district boundaries ran along county lines and were not easily manipulated.

In Virginia, a state "thoroughly schooled in politics," 24 senatorial districts were created. Though no county was divided, counties were combined in ways that gave the state's most powerful political coalition an advantage. "The gerrymander was formed," according to Griffith, "by throwing large numbers of the opposition into a district and far fewer inhabitants of the dominant faction into other districts."[26]

It's worth noting that in both the colonial assemblies and in the early state legislatures, multimember districts (i.e., districts with more than one representative) were much more common than single-member districts. Writing in 1955 about the prevalence of multimember districts in the contemporary state legislatures, Maurice Klain argued, "Neither the multiple district nor its widespread use is an emergent of recent times. It is the single-member district that stands outside of history, an alien to the past, a new-fangled and upstart thing."[27] As we'll see later, single-member districts would become the norm first (and quite early) for Congress and then, following the voting rights revolution of the 1960s, in state legislatures. That development is important both for the creation of "majority-minority" districts in the latter half of the twentieth century and for the potential for radically reforming the way representatives are elected.

In addition to populating their legislatures with representatives, the new states also had to send representatives to Congress. Two alternatives faced the new states; they could elect all of their representatives statewide, using the "general-ticket" system, or they could elect representatives by district (most likely one per district though multimember districts were also an option). Some politicians recognized that the choice of system would have implications for political power (see the case of New Jersey below). Nevertheless, Zagarri tells us that "most of the original thirteen states had, by the second round of [federal] elections, settled into the plan they would continue to use until 1842, when Congress passed a law requiring district elections."[28]

One state that was not consistent in its use of a districting system was New Jersey. Politicians there "viewed the electoral method as a partisan tool to be used at will to maximize their party's advantage."[29] Federalists, initially the dominant party in the state, favored electing the entire congressional delegation at-large, or statewide, in 1788. Republicans tried, and failed, to introduce district plans in 1792 and 1794. However, by the end of the century Federalists were losing support throughout the state and so opted for what Zagarri calls a "vastly inequitable districting plan" in 1798.[30] Even under such a system, the Federalists lost three of the five seats in the 1798 elections. As a result, Federalists in the state legislature passed an at-large plan for 1800. This time, however, they lost all five seats. Now Republicans, widely popular throughout the state, supported the at-large system and passed general-ticket plans in 1803, 1806, and 1807. After a brief attempt by Federalists in 1812 to control elections by passing a new plan that divided the state into three congressional districts with two members each, Republicans were able to re-establish at-large elections, which were used (with one brief exception) until 1842.[31]

As with the decision to base representation on either territory or population, Zagarri found that state size influenced the decision to hold at-large versus district elections for Congress. Small states tended to favor at-large elections because interests and attitudes were thought to be homogeneous in relatively small areas. Representatives could, it was argued, know the entire state well enough to represent it effectively in Congress. Large states, with potentially great variation in geography as well as in values and interests, opted for district elections. In districts, it was argued, representatives could be more responsive than they could be while representing an entire state.[32]

Those states opting for district elections had to establish district boundaries. Newly created congressional districts would become, in the words of one politician at the time, "a new species of political society."[33] Legislators would preserve existing political units, like towns and counties, and, generally speaking, they tried to keep population sizes between districts equal.[34] Nevertheless, "state legislators still lacked a rule that would help them determine where within the state to draw district lines."[35] Upon what basis would geographical areas be placed together in a district? One option was a newly developing phenomenon, namely, partisan attachment.

In some states, this led to attempts, or fear of attempts, to gerrymander the districts. In Virginia, for example, there were concerns that the very first congressional elections would be fought in gerrymandered districts. Federalists warned that Patrick Henry, perhaps the most powerful politician in the state (after George Washington) and a staunch Anti-Federalist, was attempting to construct district maps that would give his fellow partisans an advantage in elections for Congress. James Madison's district, in particular, was allegedly drawn in such a way as to prevent him from winning a seat. Griffith examines this charge in great detail and concludes that Madison's congressional district was not gerrymandered; even if it had been, Madison prevailed in the 1789 election.[36]

Griffith maintains that the first gerrymandered congressional districts in the United States, in actuality, were those in New York. In the third congressional district in 1789, for instance, "It is very probable that part of Federal Westchester (County) was added to Anti-federal Dutchess (County) in order to make the district Federalist."[37] The addition of five towns from Westchester to the third district was not for the purpose of equalizing district populations since the third district had a larger population than the surrounding districts in the 1790 census.

There were, it should be said, rudimentary efforts to prevent gerrymandering during this period. The Pennsylvania constitution of 1790 prohibited legislators from splitting either counties or the city of Philadelphia in the creation of state senate districts. Furthermore, only adjoining counties could form multi-county districts. Of course, as Griffith points out, gerrymandering might still occur in the form of grouping (rather than dividing) counties based on their voters' partisan proclivities. Nevertheless, "the clause concerning division of political units had been incorporated in the constitution in 1790 because 'it was supposed that it would prevent gerrymandering.'"[38] It's worth noting, however, that no such rule governed the drawing of congressional district lines and, indeed, Griffith suggests that congressional districts were gerrymandered twice before the end of the eighteenth century.[39]

Tennessee and Kentucky would follow the Keystone State's lead within the decade by enacting some limited prohibitions on gerrymandering.[40] Nevertheless, gerrymandering was fairly widespread in the first few decades of the American republic. The most famous case, of course, was Massachusetts in 1812. But prior to that, as Griffith concludes,

> several thoroughgoing gerrymanders had been put into operation and others had been attempted. The chief field of their operation had been New York, Pennsylvania, Virginia, and New Jersey. The principle of the gerrymander seems to have been generally understood by law-makers and was frequently practiced.[41]

The Massachusetts redistricting of 1812 is the incident that gave gerrymandering its name. Though the state had been reliably Federalist since the ratification of the Constitution, the Democratic-Republicans took control of all branches of the state government in 1811. In order to preserve their new-found power, they immediately set about redrawing the 18 state senate districts. These districts were particularly important not only for state legislative purposes but because of the role played by state senators in selecting US senators and (potentially) presidential electors.

Griffith writes that the Democratic-Republicans (otherwise known as either Democrats or Republicans), "went to the greatest extremes in outlining districts."[42] To begin with, rather than base representation on taxes that had already been collected, as was the usual basis for apportionment, the Democrats used taxes to be assessed in the future. This allowed them to exaggerate valuations in some areas and underrate assessments elsewhere. The result, which Griffith maintains was "a very arbitrary scheme of assessment and apportionment," was enhanced representation for Democratic-Republican areas and diminished representation for Federalist strongholds.[43]

Counties, which had not been divided into senatorial districts prior to this redistricting, were now divided in seemingly arbitrary (though, in reality, partisan) ways. In previous years, counties had been arbitrarily divided in congressional districts. Even then, however, "the division lines in counties generally took a straight direction and avoided all fantastic outlines and figures."[44] In the 1812 redistricting, county boundaries "were entirely disregarded" in drawing senate district lines.[45]

In the election that followed the infamous gerrymander, 29 Democratic-Republicans won state senate seats while only 11 Federalists were victorious. This lopsided outcome occurred despite the fact Federalists had received more votes than the Democrats (51,766 to 50,164).[46] Furthermore, the voters of the state selected a Federalist candidate for governor and gave the Federalists a majority of 429 to 321 in the state's lower house.[47] Clearly, the gerrymandered state senate districts accomplished what the Democrats had hoped they would.

In addition to delivering the state senate to the Democrats, the 1812 gerrymander also provoked an intense public backlash. The Democratic-Republican governor who signed the districting legislation, Elbridge Gerry, took the brunt of the criticism even though it is said that he had opposed the gerrymander. It's worth quoting at length an early biographer of Gerry's on the Governor's attitude toward the plan.

> To the governour the project of this law was exceedingly disagreeable. He urged to his friends strong arguments against its policy as well as its effects. After it had passed both houses, he hesitated to give it his signature, and meditated to return it to the legislature with his objections to its becoming a law, but being satisfied that it conformed to the constitution, he doubted whether against precedents to the contrary, the private opinion of a governour on a mere question of propriety or policy, would justify the interposition of his negative, and he accordingly permitted it to pass. Notwithstanding his hostility to the project and his repugnance to its passage, the opposition had the address to have him in the public mind considered the author of the plan, and to affix to it a variation of his name to encourage the belief that it was his own individual invention.[48]

One Boston newspaper produced a cartoon depicting one of the senate districts as a salamander (see figure 2.1). Given Gerry's alleged authorship of the map, the newspaper dubbed the district a "Gerry-mander." Such mocking was mild compared to some of the responses Gerry received. After the Governor's thanksgiving proclamation was issued in October of 1812, a broadside from one opponent "surpassed in intemperance of expression whatever before had been considered the limits of political severity."[49] Indeed, the Governor even received anonymous threats.[50]

Though held in the same gerrymandered districts, the 1813 state senate elections reversed the previous year's results. Federalists took 29 seats to the Democrats' 11. Once in office, the Federalists promptly repealed the gerrymandered map.[51]

The partisan activity of the Massachusetts Democratic-

Figure 2.1. The Original Gerrymander
Source: Elkanah Tisdale / Public domain.

Republicans in 1812 was not an isolated incident in the early part of the nineteenth century. Erik Engstrom analyzed the vote-to-seat translation in congressional elections in the first four decades of that century and found significant partisan bias in the redistricting plans of the Democratic-Republicans. Between 1802 and 1820, the bias in those plans was worth 8.66 percentage points, meaning that a statewide vote of 50 percent would give Democratic-Republicans 58.66 percent of the congressional seats. That bias jumps to an astonishing 17.92 percentage points between 1822 and 1840.[52] The bias in plans drawn by the Federalists (in 1802–1820) and, later, the National Republicans/Whigs (in 1822–1840) did not differ significantly from zero, meaning there was essentially no bias in those plans. In both cases, Engstrom notes that there were likely too few plans drawn by Federalists or National Republicans/Whigs for the small amount of bias to reach statistical significance.[53]

Engstrom not only examined partisan bias in the districting plans of the first half of the nineteenth century, but he analyzed the electoral responsiveness of those plans. Electoral responsiveness, which is sometimes referred to as the "swing ratio," is "the change in a party's aggregate seat share given a 1 percent change in their vote share."[54] A high level of electoral responsiveness indicates that there is a large number of highly competitive districts in a plan; that is, a small shift in the statewide vote will lead to a large swing in seats. A low responsiveness value indicates a large number of safe seats. Engstrom found that Democratic-Republican plans between 1802 and 1840 had relatively low levels of electoral responsiveness. The partisan strategy in the early nineteenth century, it would appear, was to protect as many (safe) seats as possible at the expense of potentially gaining additional seats in competitive districts.[55]

Interestingly, Engstrom shows that gerrymandering played a considerable role in the legislative success of the Louisiana Purchase. Following the 1801 apportionment, Democratic-Republicans controlled the redistricting process in states that gained 37 new House seats; in the 1802 congressional elections, they captured 26 of those seats.[56] Subsequently, the Federalists narrowly failed on two key votes to stop Jefferson's plan to acquire the Louisiana Territory. "Absent the additional seats picked up in the 1802 round of redistricting," concludes Engstrom, "Republicans likely would have failed to defeat the Federalist attempts to block the purchase."[57]

Gerrymandering, then, was a widespread and consequential phenomenon in the first several decades of the nineteenth century. It would, undoubtedly, remain so as the century progressed. Indeed, a significant change to congressional elections in 1842 would increase the opportunities for gerrymandering.

Redistricting in the Mid- to Late Nineteenth Century

Recall that, originally, states could choose to elect members of Congress either statewide (i.e., on a general ticket) or in districts. "Between 1789 and 1840," reports Engstrom, "over a quarter of the states in any given Congress used the general-ticket method of electing representatives, yielding an average of 15 percent of the House membership."[58] Recall, too, that while most states chose a method and kept with it throughout the years, it was possible to change methods. When a change occurred, it was typically because it served the political interests of the dominant party in the state.

In the 1840 elections, the Whig Party won – for the first time ever – control of both chambers of Congress and the presidency. This moment in American political history was the mid-point of what scholars refer to as the second party system in the United States.[59] It was a period of intense partisan competition.

Given the results of the 1840 census, it appeared that reapportionment would add House seats to Democratic states using the general ticket while reducing seats in general-ticket states where Whigs performed well. The Whigs realized that they might be able to win at least a few seats in Democratic states if those states were to utilize single-member districts.[60] Of course, Democratic legislators in those states had no incentive to switch to single-member districts. As a result, the new Whig majority in Congress would have to take matters into their own hands.

In drafting the Apportionment Bill of 1842, the Whigs reduced the number of representatives in the House and, more importantly for our purposes, imposed geographically contiguous, single-member districts on all states with more than one representative. Engstrom maintains that the latter reform was little more than an attempt by Whigs "to try and maintain their majority in the House."[61] Other scholars, however, have argued that the debates over the Apportionment Bill of 1842 included competing theories of representation.[62] Regardless of how strategic the changes might have been, the new system did not prevent the crushing defeat of the Whigs in the 1844 elections. Nevertheless, the requirement that congressional elections be held in single-member districts was maintained and it has remained in place ever since (with some minor exceptions).

In the middle of the nineteenth century, states redrew district boundaries at will. Though some states went long stretches of time without drawing new district lines, many redrew lines frequently. According to Engstrom, "Between 1862 and 1896, there was only one election year in which at least one state did not redraw its congressional districts."[63] Of course, the addition or loss of House seats following the decennial apportionment was likely to force states to redistrict. However, the Apportionment Act of 1872 allowed a state gaining seats to maintain its previous map and to elect the additional representatives at-large until the state adopted a redistricting plan. For states that lost House seats following the census, the 1882 Apportionment Act allowed the entire congressional delegation to be elected at-large (i.e., on the "general ticket") until a new map could be drawn.[64] Both of these provisions would remain in force until Congress finally banned the use of multimember districts in 1967.[65]

Engstrom's analysis shows that from 1840 to 1900, unprompted redistricting – that is, redistricting that happened outside the census cycle or, following a census, when a state failed to gain or lose seats – tended to occur when a party that had been out of power took control of state government and the current map had been produced by the party that had just lost control of the government.[66] From 1870 to 1940, in nearly 40 percent of the cases in which a state gained seats following reapportionment, they would elect their new members in at-large elections. Two factors help explain a state's likelihood of doing so. When either control of state government was divided or the party in control of a unified government commanded a large share of the statewide congressional vote (i.e., the party was confident it could win the statewide vote), at-large elections were utilized to fill newly apportioned seats.[67] Under those conditions, redrawing district maps was either difficult (under divided government) or was politically unappealing (to a strong party in control of unified government). Finally, there were not many cases of states losing seats following apportionment after 1880, when states were permitted to use the general ticket to temporarily elect their entire congressional delegations statewide. Nevertheless, the behavior of states in at least a few of those cases suggests that "the strategic deployment of a general-ticket election dramatically strengthened the hand of the party with the strongest electoral future."[68] The conclusion to be drawn from Engstrom's analysis is that, when they were able, parties chose a method of electing members of Congress that was likely to give the party an advantage.

In fact, in the last half of the nineteenth century, partisan districting plans appear to have been successful in providing an advantage for the party drawing the maps. Between 1840 and 1900, the difference between a partisan map and a bipartisan map, according to Engstrom, was a partisan gain of 15 percent of a state's congressional delegation on average.[69] Switching control of the map from one party to the other would produce a partisan swing of 30 percent of the state's congressional seats. When aggregated nationally, the effect of gerrymandering on state delegations might very well influence the partisan balance of seats in the House of Representatives. Indeed, Engstrom found that in two elections – 1878 and 1888 – control of the House was determined, at least in part, by successful gerrymanders in Ohio and Missouri (for Democrats) and Pennsylvania (for Republicans), respectively.[70]

Though gerrymandering is viewed by many citizens today as a tool for reducing competition in legislative districts (by, for example, protecting incumbents), gerrymandered districts could just as easily be used to increase competition. The redistricting choices of partisan mapmakers will be discussed later in the book. For now, suffice it say that districting plans can either maximize the number of safe seats in a state (i.e., districts that one party or the other can easily win) or they can maximize the number of marginal seats (i.e., districts that either party could potentially win). In the late nineteenth century, parties appear to have taken the latter approach. This is not to say that parties weren't trying to gain a partisan advantage. It simply means that, rather than concede a few safe seats to the other party while protecting the majority for themselves, the party in control of redistricting tried to maximize the number of seats they might conceivably win. This strategy, as Engstrom notes, was risky. "With so many districts on the knife-edge," he explains, "a slight shift in the vote to the opposite party could spell electoral doom."[71]

Engstrom's evidence suggests that parties in the late nineteenth century followed a seat-maximization, rather than a seat-protection, strategy.[72] One of the consequences of such a strategy was that swing ratios in states – or the change in the percentage of legislative seats controlled by a party given a change in the percentage of votes received[73] – increased significantly following redistricting.[74] In what was already a highly competitive era, gerrymandering contributed to the dramatic electoral volatility.

Candidate decisions about entering (and exiting) races were also affected by redistricting. When new maps were drawn in a state, incumbent members of Congress were less likely to seek re-election.[75] In addition, Jamie Carson and his colleagues found that "the redrawing of district lines in the late nineteenth century was strongly related to candidate recruitment and entry."[76] Specifically, as districts were drawn to favor one party over the other, candidates with electoral experience (or "quality candidates") were more likely to enter a congressional race.

Redistricting in the Early to Mid-Twentieth Century

"[I]f the issue in the 19th century was too much redistricting," writes Engstrom, "in the 20th century it became too little redistricting."[77] Among the consequences of this development was the professionalization of members of Congress who, in their increasing electoral safety, began to build long congressional careers. That professionalization, in turn, resulted in the modernization of the House of Representatives.

Why did the frequency of redistricting decline in the twentieth century? Engstrom attributes it to the rapid decline of partisan competition in the states.[78] The Civil War had produced a sectionalism in American politics that was firmly entrenched in much of the country by 1900. The South, of course, was solidly controlled by the Democratic Party while the North had become thoroughly Republican. Writing in the middle of the twentieth century, the renowned political scientist V. O. Key, Jr. concluded, "in about only a dozen states do the two major parties compete on a fairly even basis."[79] Without party competition, there wasn't likely to be regular turnover in control of state legislatures; without partisan turnover of the legislature, there was no incentive to redraw district maps in the vast majority of states.

Engstrom illustrates the static nature of redistricting plans in the early twentieth century by calculating the average age of state maps of congressional districts. Between 1850 and 1890, the average age of such maps was under ten years. Between 1890 and 1920, the average age was between 12 and 15 years. In 1930, the average leapt to 21 years and in 1960 it reached 22 years.[80]

Urbanization in the early part of the twentieth century also contributed to the decline in redistricting.[81] Rural interests in state legislatures and in Congress opposed any efforts to shift representation to the cities. In 1920, this rural–urban divide reached a boiling point. The 1920 census found that, for the first time ever, a majority of Americans lived in urban areas. Members of Congress from rural areas questioned the accuracy of the census and helped to prevent Congress from passing an apportionment bill for that decade, the first and only time that reapportionment didn't occur following the census.[82] Thus, for 20 years congressional district maps remained unchanged. Even after 1930, when apportionment resumed, state legislatures often refused to draw district maps to reflect population shifts in their states.

Infrequent redistricting and the migration of Americans into cities meant that constituency sizes became vastly unequal. In

Congress and, especially, in state legislatures, rural legislators represented far fewer constituents than did urban legislators. In California in 1960, for example, the largest state Senate district, consisting of Los Angeles County, had a population of 6,038,771, while the population in the smallest district, containing three counties in or near the Sierra Nevada mountains, was 14,196.[83]

There were at least two problems with such inequality. One was that individual voters in districts with extraordinary numbers of constituents had less voting power than those in smaller districts. Because more votes were needed to win a seat in larger districts, each vote was worth less than were votes in smaller districts (where it took fewer votes to win). Another problem was that, in the aggregate, the inequality of district populations meant representation disproportionately favored smaller districts. Because smaller districts were almost always rural, the interests of those living in rural areas were disproportionately represented. Indeed, rural representatives very often made up a majority of a state legislature, or a congressional delegation, even though a majority of the state's population lived in urban areas. Those rural representatives, in turn, could squelch attempts to equalize representation between urban and rural districts.

Stephen Ansolabehere and James Snyder consider the attempt to preserve unequal district populations, or malapportionment, to be a form of gerrymandering. "If gerrymandering was the genus," they write, "malapportionment was the species – and before 1965, its most powerful and common kind."[84] For Ansolabehere and Snyder, malapportionment "as a form of gerrymandering, manifested itself in three ways."[85] First, legislators could draw districts with unequal population in an attempt to preserve (or obtain) a majority of seats for their own party. Second, legislators might change the state constitution to create favorable apportionment criteria. And, third, as noted above, legislators could simply refuse to redistrict following the census, allowing district populations to become more and more unequal.[86]

Malapportionment would be challenged in several important court cases in the 1960s. Indeed, gerrymandering itself would be the focus of a number of legal battles in the latter half of the twentieth century. The next chapter summarizes the key decisions issued by the Supreme Court and explores the current legal status of gerrymandering.

Conclusion

This chapter briefly reviewed the ways legislative districts in America have evolved over time. In the colonial era, assembly districts were designed to represent geographical areas, not populations. That didn't preclude the manipulation of district lines; it just meant that, to do so, the boundaries of towns and counties had to be altered.

As states formed legislatures, following independence from Great Britain, some began using districts to represent people. In addition, some states began using single-member, as opposed to multimember, districts. This required district lines to be drawn with more regularity and it meant that gerrymandering of those lines was possible. Indeed, the earliest gerrymanders in the United States date to the late 1700s.

The second party system in the United States, which occurred in the middle of the nineteenth century, was characterized by fervent competition between the parties. To gain electoral advantage, parties used districts as political weapons. Unprompted redistricting in states often took place multiple times in a decade. This practice of frequent redrawing of district lines continued into the late nineteenth century.

The sectionalism that emerged following Reconstruction meant that, in most states, party competition declined dramatically. As a result, redistricting became less frequent. In fact, to avoid accounting for population shifts to urban areas, many states simply stopped redrawing legislative district lines. Consequently, by the middle of the twentieth century, districts in most states were highly unequal in terms of population size. It would take a legal revolution, which we examine in the next chapter, to transform redistricting into the process we use today.

If there is one lesson to be learned from this review of the history of districting in America it's that gerrymandering is an almost inevitable strategy in the battle for political power. When political actors are in charge of creating electoral districts, they'll design those districts in the most politically advantageous way possible. The only way to curtail such activity is to place legal limits on the ability to engage in it. As the chapters that follow suggest, this can be done in a variety of ways. Nevertheless, there is no magic formula for drawing perfectly neutral district lines (whatever those might be).

CHAPTER 3

The Legal Status of Gerrymandering

By the middle of the twentieth century, malapportionment in state legislative and congressional districts had become too large a problem to ignore. Yet state legislators, many of whom represented malapportioned districts, did just that; they ignored the problem. Stephen Ansolabehere and James Snyder have described the circumstances at the time quite distinctly. "Demand for representation intensified with the continued growth of urban and suburban communities," they write,

> but the political system seemed incapable of righting itself. State legislatures resisted reapportionment; executives could not force the issue; and majorities of the states' voters, fearing domination by the largest cities, chose to have unequal legislative representation. One possible corrective to malapportionment remained – the courts.[1]

This chapter reviews the fate of malapportionment and gerrymandering in the courts. It begins by describing the "reapportionment revolution" of the 1960s, which prohibited malapportionment of legislative districts and established the principle of "one-person, one-vote," or equality of representation. It then considers legal challengers to gerrymanders based on race and, eventually, based on partisanship. It concludes by explaining the current legal status of gerrymandering in the United States.

The redistricting process is now governed by a set of standards that were not present 60 years ago. As a result, legislative districts are much fairer, in many respects, than they were before the middle of the twentieth century. Nevertheless, partisan gerrymandering is alive and well and appears to have been sanctioned by the Supreme Court. To the extent that partisan gerrymandering threatens the fairness of elections, whether in constitutional or philosophical terms, the redistricting process remains in need of reform.

The Apportionment Cases

When three attorneys filed a lawsuit in federal court challenging malapportionment in Tennessee on May 18, 1959, it had been almost 60 years since the state had last reapportioned state legislative districts.[2] The heart of the legal argument the attorneys hoped to make was that, by failing to reapportion the state's legislative districts, Tennessee was violating the Equal Protection and Due Process Clauses of the Fourteenth Amendment to the United States Constitution. The three-judge panel that would hear the case, however, limited the argument to whether or not the courts could adjudicate the matter.[3]

The question of the courts' jurisdiction in reapportionment and redistricting cases had been answered by the Supreme Court several years earlier, in 1946, in a 4–3 decision in *Colegrove v. Green*.[4] In that case, petitioners sued the state of Illinois for violating the equal protection of the voting rights of some citizens (particularly those in urban areas like Chicago) by having refused to reapportion US House districts in over 40 years. In his majority opinion in *Colegrove*, Justice Felix Frankfurter argued that those who brought the lawsuit were asking the Court to do "what is beyond its competence to grant."[5] Not only did the Court lack the ability to redraw district maps, it would be a bad idea for it to wade into the politics of reapportionment and redistricting.

"Courts," wrote Frankfurter, "ought not to enter this political thicket."[6]

With the *Colegrove* decision serving as precedent, the three-judge panel considering the Tennessee lawsuit dismissed the case. Though they believed the legislature was "guilty of a clear violation of the state constitution" and that the violation was "a serious one which should be corrected without delay," they nonetheless felt that courts were unable to offer a remedy in what was, at root, a political controversy.[7] The petitioners appealed to the Supreme Court, which agreed in November of 1960 to hear the case of *Baker v. Carr*.[8]

Oral argument in *Baker* took place in April of 1961. The appellants maintained that Tennessee was violating the Fourteenth Amendment and, as such, federal intervention was required. The respondents, defending the state of Tennessee, claimed the federal courts simply had no jurisdiction in the case.[9] When the Supreme Court justices conferenced about the case, they were deadlocked 4–4 on whether or not to reverse the lower court ruling, with Justice Potter Stewart abstaining. Justice Stewart wasn't particularly concerned about the Court entering a political dispute but he had doubts about the substantive argument made by the appellants (i.e., that Tennessee was violating some citizens' equal protection rights). He asked that the case be reargued and the rest of the Court agreed to hear another round of arguments in October of 1961.[10]

In the months following the April hearing, the appellants were able to gather newly released census data to show how malapportioned Tennessee's legislative districts had become. The government used that data to argue in its amicus brief that "the legislative apportionment in Tennessee is so grossly discriminatory as to violate the Fourteenth Amendment and that judicial relief is available against this violation."

Furthermore, the government argued that the protections against discrimination in the Fourteenth Amendment do not apply only to race but "extend to arbitrary and capricious action against other groups." Finally, the brief maintained that when determining a standard to apply in cases such as this, "the starting point must be *per capita* equality of representation, a fundamental American ideal."[11]

When the second round of oral arguments had ended, the justices conferenced almost immediately. Justice Warren suggested a narrow decision that would reverse the lower court "solely on jurisdiction."[12] Still, eight of the nine justices were of the same opinion they had held after the first round of arguments. Justice Stewart, however, broke the deadlock by agreeing to support the narrow judgment to reverse. (The final vote would be 6–2 as Justice Clark later switched his vote to join the majority and Justice Whitaker failed to participate in the final decision as he had been hospitalized for depression.[13])

Justice Brennan wrote the majority opinion in *Baker*, which he delivered in March of 1962. In it, he argued "that jurisdiction existed, that the complaint stated a justiciable cause of action, and that the appellants possessed standing to maintain the action."[14] The distinction between jurisdiction and justiciability need not be explicated here, though it is the fact that apportionment cases would henceforth be considered justiciable that makes *Baker v. Carr* a landmark decision. Brennan explained that justiciability is concerned with whether "the duty asserted can be judicially identified and its breach judicially determined, and whether protection for the right asserted can be judicially molded."[15] In deciding that apportionment cases were, indeed, justiciable, the Court almost immediately found itself enmeshed in the political thicket about which Justice Frankfurter had warned.

Within a month of the *Baker* decision, apportionment lawsuits had been filed in at least 22 states.[16] The first subsequent case to be heard by the Supreme Court was *Gray v. Sanders*, a challenge to Georgia's primary system, which used the county-unit rule.[17] In that system, counties were allotted a certain number of unit-votes and the candidate winning a plurality of ballots cast in a county would win all of the county's unit-votes. "The problem," according to Ansolabehere and Snyder, "was that unit-votes were not proportionate to population, and Fulton and DeKalb counties [in which parts of the city of Atlanta are located] had many fewer unit-votes than their populations warranted."[18] In other words, the value of a vote differed based on one's county of residence.

In a 7–1 decision, the Supreme Court held that the county-unit rule violated the constitutional rights of some Georgians. Writing for the majority, Justice Douglas coined a now famous phrase. Political equality, Douglas asserted, "can only mean one thing – one person, one vote."[19] This new standard for electoral democracy in the United States – one person, one vote – resonated deeply with Americans and has become almost synonymous with democracy itself.

Two more cases, *Wesberry v. Sanders* and *Reynolds v. Sims*, dealt with malapportionment in US House districts and in state legislative districts, respectively.[20] Decided in 1964, both cases combined several similar lawsuits into one. In *Wesberry*, the Court ruled that "the command of Article I, Section 2 [of the US Constitution], that Representatives be chosen 'by the People of the several states' means that as nearly as is practicable one man's vote in a congressional election is to be worth as much as another's."[21] In *Reynolds*, the Court applied similar logic to state legislative elections. The Equal Protection Clause, wrote Chief Justice Warren in his majority opinion, "demands no less than substantially equal state legislative representation for all citizens, of all places as well as of all races."[22]

On the same day the decision in *Reynolds* was announced, the Court also announced its ruling in *Lucas v. Colorado*.[23] In that case, Colorado's malapportioned state senate was at issue. Interestingly, the apportionment system that led to unequal representation had been accepted by voters in a ballot initiative, creating a potentially powerful argument in support of that system. Nevertheless, the Court disapproved of the Colorado apportionment arguing, "An individual's constitutionally protected right to cast an equally weighted vote cannot be denied even by a vote of a majority of the State's electorate."[24]

Interestingly, in its *Reynolds* and *Lucas* decisions, the Court rejected the "federal analogy," whereby state senates were thought to be analogous to the federal Senate. The argument from the federal analogy was that if representation in the federal Senate could be based on something other than population, so could representation in the upper chamber of a bi-cameral state legislature. In the previous year, the Court had rejected a similar argument in *Gray v. Sanders* analogizing the county-unit rule to the Electoral College. Now, in *Reynolds* and *Lucas*, it was rejecting the Senate analogy. While the federal government is a federation of states, states are not federations of counties. Indeed, as Richard Cortner explains, "Local units of government have never been sovereign entities as were the original states which formed the Union and received equal representation in the Senate."[25] Furthermore, the Court noted in *Reynolds*, the "Founding Fathers clearly had no intention of establishing a pattern or model for the apportionment of seats in state legislatures when the system of representation in the Federal Congress was adopted."[26]

In 1964, the Supreme Court would decide a number of other apportionment cases. In fact, "In just two weeks, the Justices had declared unconstitutional the apportionments in seventeen states."[27] More than that, in just two years the Court had created a revolution in the way Americans were represented in state legislatures and in the US House of Representatives. From that moment forward, equality was the standard for apportioning districts.

Left unanswered, however, was just how equal districts had to be to pass constitutional muster. The Court dealt with this question directly in a 1973 case called *Gaffney v. Cummings*.[28] That case involved state legislative districts in Connecticut where Senate districts deviated from perfect equality by 1.81 percent and House districts deviated by 7.83 percent.[29] The Court upheld these districts and ruled that no justification by the state was required for deviations of this magnitude. In his dissent, Justice Brennan concluded, based on a review of related court decisions, "that a line has been drawn at 10% – deviations in excess of that amount are apparently acceptable only on a showing of justification by the State; deviations less than that amount require no justification whatsoever."[30] Though not intended by Brennan to serve as a rule, the ten percent threshold continues to apply to state legislative districts today. It should be noted, however, that it does not serve as a "safe harbor." That is, district deviations under ten percent can be challenged in court if those districts discriminate against a group of voters.

Article I, Section 2 of the Constitution governs congressional elections and stipulates that "Representatives . . . shall be apportioned among the several States . . . according to their respective Numbers." In *Wesberry*, the Court interpreted that to mean that congressional districts must be drawn on the basis of equal population. In *Karcher v. Daggett* (1983), the Court required such districts to be as close to equal as possible.[31] Even a total deviation of 0.6984 percent (or 3,674 people), as was the situation in the New Jersey case under consideration in *Karcher*, would be suspect as long as those challenging the district plan could show that a good-faith effort could create a more equal plan and that the state could not show that a legitimate state objective was served by the unequal districts.[32]

Apportionment, then, seemed settled as a matter of law by the mid-1980s. State legislative districts had to be substantially equal in size while congressional districts had to be strictly equal. In 2016, however, another apportionment-related legal challenge emerged.[33] Plaintiffs in Texas questioned the use of total population, as opposed to voting-eligible population, during the apportionment process for state legislative districts. They argued that districts with large numbers of immigrants who are ineligible to vote gave voters in those districts disproportionate power compared to voters in districts with fewer immigrants. This, they argued, is a violation of the Equal Protection Clause because *voters* are not treated equally. As a result, they wanted the Court to prohibit the use of total population for apportionment.

A unanimous Court rejected the plaintiffs' argument; it is constitutionally permissible to use total population for apportionment. However, the Court did not rule that total population is the only acceptable method of apportionment. Indeed, the opinions of two concurring justices suggested that states could use alternative methods, including the number of eligible voters.[34] Determining the "citizen voting-age population" (i.e., voting-eligible population) for use in districting seems to have been the purpose of the Trump Administration's attempt to put a citizenship question on the 2020 census.[35] Should states begin using voting-eligible population for districting, this issue will surely find itself back in court.

Racial Gerrymandering Cases

Following the "reapportionment revolution" of the mid-1960s, state legislators could no longer use malapportionment to accomplish their political goals. Nevertheless, they had other tools at their disposal. The primary tool was, of course, gerrymandering. This was a more subtle approach – a scalpel compared to the axe of malapportionment – but it was no less effective. In fact, it might have been far more valuable to legislators who wanted to manipulate elections without appearing to do so. District lines can be drawn in countless ways, so placing a line here rather than there can seem, at first glance, to be an arbitrary choice. In addition, there is no immediately obvious metric to use in finding bias in district maps (in the way unequal population sizes reveal malapportionment).

Though gerrymandering could be used to reduce the influence of any group of voters, it was initially used as a means of discriminating against non-white voters. Interestingly, the first case to make an argument against gerrymandering on the basis of racial discrimination preceded *Baker* by several months. Indeed, when *Gomillion v. Lightfoot* (1960) was before the Court, a gerrymandering case might well have been viewed as part of the "political thicket" to be avoided according to *Colgrove*.

Gomillion concerned district boundaries for the city of Tuskegee, Alabama.[36] At the request of city leaders, the Alabama legislature had altered the municipal boundaries of Tuskegee to exclude virtually all blacks from the city. The case could have been decided on either Fourteenth Amendment due process and equal protection grounds or on the grounds that the Fifteenth Amendment protects voting rights based on race.[37] Though either would have satisfied the plaintiffs, the former would have put *Colgrove* in jeopardy. Thus, when the Court decided, unanimously, that the Alabama legislature had violated the rights of Tuskegee's black residents, it relied upon the Fifteenth Amendment to do so (though Justice Whitaker's concurring opinion indicated that he would have overturned the Tuskegee map as a violation of the Fourteenth Amendment).[38]

Though the *Gomillion* decision made it clear that the denial of voting rights based on race was not legal, civil rights activists feared continued discrimination with respect to voting rights, and for good reason. Attempts to prevent blacks and other non-white citizens from voting continued into the 1960s. As a result, the Voting Rights Act of 1965 (VRA) was enacted to protect those voters. It did so in several ways. For our purposes, the most important of these are Sections 2, 4 and 5 of the VRA.

Section 2 reiterated the protections found in the Fifteenth Amendment to the Constitution, stating: "No voting qualification or prerequisite to voting, or standard, practice, or procedure shall be imposed or applied by any State or political subdivision to deny or abridge the right of any citizen of the United States to vote on account of race or color."[39] A 1982 amendment to Section 2 added language that reduced the burden plaintiffs faced in establishing voter discrimination.

Section 4 of the VRA established criteria by which states and localities would be covered by Section 5 of the VRA. Essentially, covered states and localities were those with a history of discriminatory practices. Section 5, in turn, required covered states and localities to get "preclearance" for any changes to voting procedures. That is, before new voting laws were enacted in states or localities covered by the VRA, those laws had to be approved by the federal government. Preclearance was granted after either an administrative review by the US Attorney General or a lawsuit in the US District Court for the District of Columbia.

Given the revisions to Section 2 of the VRA in 1982, those seeking to challenge state redistricting plans on the basis of racial discrimination faced a lower hurdle. In particular, minority voting rights could be found to have been violated based on the *effects* of a given state's laws and not only if those laws had a discriminatory *purpose* (as the Supreme Court had said was necessary in *Mobile v. Bolden* in 1980).[40] As a result, if a redistricting plan led to a dilution of minority voting power, that plan would be constitutionally suspect regardless of the intentions of the plan's authors. Since Section 2 did not demand that redistricting plans achieve precise proportionality in minority representation, Congress provided guidelines for the courts as they considered voter discrimination cases. When determining whether a redistricting plan violated the VRA, the courts were to consider the "totality of circumstances" in an electoral jurisdiction. This meant, essentially, that the history of discrimination within a jurisdiction had to be taken into account.[41]

In *Thornburg v. Gingles* (1986), the Supreme Court heard a challenge to a North Carolina redistricting plan.[42] In addition to single-member districts the plan also included several multimember districts. Those multimember districts, and one single-member state senate district, were challenged by a group of black voters who claimed that the districts made it impossible for them to elect their candidates of choice.[43] In a complex ruling in favor of the plaintiffs, the Court devised its own test for determining whether multimember districts diluted minority voting power.

The Court maintained that a plan would violate minority voting rights if the minority group in question (1) is "sufficiently large and geographically compact to constitute a majority in a single-member district;" (2) is "politically cohesive;" and (3) can "demonstrate that the white majority votes sufficiently as a bloc to enable it ... usually to defeat the minority's preferred candidate."[44] This three-pronged test, which came to be known as the *Gingles* test, raised a number of complex issues.[45] Among the questions the test raised, "the

most important but in a way the most maddening and problematic of all," according to Richard Scher, Jon Mills, and John
Hotaling, is "what does *Gingles* require, what does it permit or
allow, and what does it forbid?"[46]

In the 1991–2 redistricting cycle, many states took *Gingles*
to require the creation of majority-minority districts, that is,
districts in which a majority of the voters are racial minorities. These districts often took odd shape, and occasionally
took extremely peculiar shape, which raised questions about
the legitimacy of the districts. Two such districts for congressional seats, perhaps not coincidentally in North Carolina,
were challenged in *Shaw v. Reno* (1993).[47] The plaintiffs in
the case, a group of white voters, argued that the districts con-
stituted racial gerrymandering and, thus, violated their voting
rights.

Though the Court did not reach a decision on the merits
of the case (i.e., whether the districts violated the rights of
the plaintiffs), it reversed and remanded the case to the district court, which had dismissed the plaintiff's challenge. In so
doing, the Court raised questions about the "bizarre" nature of
at least one of the districts. Writing for the majority (in a 5–4
decision), Justice O'Connor questioned whether there was a
rational basis for the districts, beyond race, and argued,

> A reapportionment plan that includes in one district individu-
> als who belong to the same race, but who are otherwise widely
> separated by geographical and political boundaries, and who
> may have little in common with one another but the color of
> their skin, bears an uncomfortable resemblance to political
> apartheid.[48]

Majority-minority districts were not necessarily forbidden by
Shaw. However, the barrier to creating constitutionally acceptable majority-minority districts had apparently been set quite
high. Unfortunately, the Court did not offer clear guidance as

to what was, and was not, acceptable with respect to creating districts that enhanced minority voting rights.[49] It seemed to suggest that bizarrely drawn districts are problematic, but it never explained what makes a district bizarrely drawn.

Not surprisingly, more lawsuits followed. In *Miller v. Johnson* (1995), the Court struck down Georgia's majority-minority Eleventh Congressional District.[50] In doing so, the Court was less interested in the shape of the district than with the intention of those who created the district. The main conclusion of *Miller* was that race cannot be the "predominant" factor motivating the drawing of district boundaries.[51]

This put mapmakers in a difficult spot. On the one hand, *Gingles* had suggested that the creation of majority-minority districts would avoid discrimination against minority voters. *Shaw* and *Miller*, on the other hand, warned those drawing lines to be careful; the shape of majority-minority districts shouldn't be too peculiar and race couldn't be the main reason for such districts.

Bush v. Vera (1996), a plurality opinion with three concurring and two dissenting opinions, did little to clarify the situation.[52] States, the Court held, could not subordinate traditional districting criteria, such as compactness, to race in drawing district lines. The three districts under consideration in *Vera* were oddly shaped and anything but compact (see figure 3.1). In addition, the Court noted that the use of sophisticated computer software allowed the state to achieve an unprecedented level of precision in terms of the racial makeup of these districts. As a result, these particular districts were unconstitutional racial gerrymanders. Similarly, in its reconsideration of two North Carolina congressional districts, which had been remanded to the District Court in *Shaw*, the Supreme Court found it constitutionally problematic that "[r]ace was the criterion that, in the State's view, could not be compromised;

Figure 3.1. Texas' 30th Congressional District (1996)

Source: Supreme Court of the United States / Public domain.

respecting communities of interest and protecting Democratic incumbents came into play only after the race-based decision had been made."[53]

Despite the rulings in *Bush* and *Shaw II*, however, race-conscious districting was not outlawed.[54] Indeed, the Court upheld the map of North Carolina's Twelfth Congressional District in *Easley v. Cromartie* (2001) just five years after *Bush* and *Shaw II*.[55] The issue in *Easley* was whether there was sufficient evidence that "race *rather than* politics *predominantly* explains" the district's boundaries.[56] The Court found that there was no such evidence in this particular case. That is, politics (i.e., partisanship), not race, seemed the driving force behind the creation of the Twelfth District and, thus, the district withstood challenge.

For a time after *Easley*, there were very few successful challenges to redistricting plans on racial gerrymandering grounds. This appeared to mean that *Easley* settled matters. "A more likely explanation," write Daniel Lowenstein and Richard Hasen,

> is that the racial gerrymandering cases of the 1990s repre-
> sented a judicial reaction (perhaps a very ham-handed one) to
> the Justice Department's extremely aggressive application of
> Section 5 of the Voting Rights Act, which provoked some state
> legislatures to take liberties with district shapes beyond what
> they typically had done previously, in order to satisfy the Justice
> Department without abandoning their other political objec-
> tives. The chastisement the Court administered to the Justice
> Department in the 1990s was sufficient to prevent a repetition
> of these events in the 2000s and are likely to be sufficient for
> that purpose in future decades.[57]

Eventually, the Court dealt with Section 5 of the VRA in an even more consequential way. In *Shelby County v. Holder* (2013), they ruled that the formula used for determining which jurisdictions were covered by the preclearance requirement (Section 4(b)) was outdated and could no longer be consti-tutionally justified.[58] Though it did not strike down Section 5 itself, the ruling in *Shelby County* rendered preclearance essentially inoperable.[59] Congress could revise and update Section 4(b) but the likelihood of that happening in an era of partisan polarization is low. As a result, states that toy with racial gerrymandering can implement their plans without pre-clearance and can be stymied only by legal challenges based on Section 2 of the VRA. Unfortunately for the plaintiffs, Section 2 lawsuits are "lengthy, expensive, and often don't yield results until after an election (or several) is over."[60]

Still, some challenges to racial gerrymandering have been successful in recent years. Recall that *Easley* had treated race and partisanship as separable characteristics and had said that race could not be the predominant factor in drawing district maps. Following the 2010 census, Republicans in many states were successful in drawing districts that were advantageous to them by creating others that were heavily populated by Black voters. When confronted with charges of gerrymandering based on race, Hasen notes that these states "defended their district lines either by claiming the districts had to be drawn the way they were in order to comply with Section 2 or Section 5 of the Voting Rights Act, or that they were political, not racial, gerrymanders under *Easley*."[61] Coming on the heels of successful challenges to several districts in Alabama (in 2015) and Virginia (in 2017), *Cooper v. Harris* (2017) considered the legality of the same two districts in North Carolina that had been the focus of *Shaw*, the First and the Twelfth.[62]

At issue in *Cooper* was whether the number of Black voters had to be increased in the First District in order to comply with Section 2 of the VRA and whether race was the predominant consideration in the Twelfth. With respect to the former, the Supreme Court was unanimous in finding that, although compliance with the VRA can be a compelling reason to draw majority-minority districts, North Carolina had not established the need to do so in this particular situation.[63] Essentially, the Court found that enough white voters in the old First District were willing to support candidates preferred by Black voters not to need additional Black voters in the district. In other words, the VRA did not require the new First District as a remedy to discrimination.[64]

In defense of the Twelfth District, the state of North Carolina maintained that the rationale behind the district's demographic makeup was partisan. It acknowledged that race had been used in the process but, given the close tie between partisan voting patterns and race, it was primarily to estimate the partisan consequences of the district. Based on *Easley*, this would be perfectly acceptable.

In a 5–3 decision based largely on evidence provided when

the case was heard in trial court, the Supreme Court ruled that North Carolina had illegally used race in drawing the boundaries of the Twelfth. In a footnote in her opinion for the majority, Justice Kagan wrote that "the sorting of voters on the grounds of their race remains suspect even if race is meant to function as a proxy for other (including political) characteristics."[65] Thus, as Hasen has put it, the Court shifted from a "race or party" view in *Easley*, whereby the question is what is the predominant factor in drawing district lines, to a "race as party" approach, whereby the Court sees any use of race, even as a surrogate for party, as dubious.[66]

The Court, then, seems to be warning mapmakers to tread lightly when it comes to using race to draw district lines. However, conservatives on the Court (with the exception of Justice Thomas, who has consistently been suspicious of the role of race in redistricting) tend to be more willing to allow the use of race as a proxy for party. As the balance on the Court shifts to the right, this may spell the end of successful challenges to gerrymanders based on race. This is why scholars like Hasen maintain that, rather than focus on the inappropriate use of race (except where the violations are egregious), voting rights advocates and redistricting reformers should adopt a "party all the time" approach.[67]

Partisan Gerrymandering Cases

Party identification is not constitutionally protected when it comes to voting the way race (Fifteenth Amendment), sex (Nineteenth Amendment), and age (Twenty-Sixth Amendment) are protected. Yet voters who are gerrymandered into the numerical minority in a given district will never be able to elect their candidates of choice. Surely one could argue that this is a violation of those voters' right to equal protection.

Recall that in *Gaffney v. Cummings* (1973) the Court dealt with the question of whether state legislative districts could deviate from strict equality. In addition, the plaintiffs in *Gaffney* challenged the state of Connecticut's "political fairness" policy, whereby legislative districts were drawn in such a way as to roughly approximate statewide support for the two major parties. In other words, the state hoped to achieve something like proportional representation with its redistricting plan.[68] The plaintiffs in the case argued that "political fairness" nonetheless amounted to a political gerrymander that gave one party an advantage and violated the equal protection rights of voters in the disadvantaged party. The Court disagreed. In so doing, however, Justice White's majority opinion noted that certain districts (and, specifically, multimember districts) "may be vulnerable, if racial *or political groups* have been fenced out of the political process and their voting strength invidiously minimized."[69] By indicating that "political groups," in addition to racial groups, might deserve protection against gerrymanders that dilute their voting strength, the Court seemed to be suggesting that partisan gerrymanders could be justiciable.[70]

In *Davis v. Bandemer* (1986), a majority of the Supreme Court confirmed that they were, indeed, willing to consider the constitutionality of partisan gerrymanders.[71] Nevertheless, the particular districting plan under consideration in *Bandemer*, namely the 1982 Indiana state legislative map, was held to be a constitutionally valid plan. Besides the justiciability of partisan gerrymanders, however, the most important part of the *Bandemer* decision was the criteria a plurality of the Court appeared to establish for deciding such cases. Unfortunately, such criteria were ambiguous and, as a result, were subject to a variety of interpretations.[72]

Perhaps the most common interpretation was that "a disadvantaged political party must prove both an intent to discriminate against it as well as an actual discriminatory effect."[73] Establishing both elements of this standard was, as one might imagine, very difficult. To begin with, we might assume that intent to disadvantage the other party is always present when partisan elected officials are in charge of drawing district boundaries. What, precisely, would count as evidence of such intent? Furthermore, the Court maintained that proving discriminatory effect required more than showing that a given party received disproportionately fewer seats in the legislature than the party's vote share would suggest. Instead, the disadvantaged party had to provide

> evidence that excluded groups have "less opportunity to participate in the political processes and to elect candidates of their choice," [or that] the electoral system substantially disadvantages certain voters in their opportunity to influence the political process effectively ... [There must be] evidence of continued frustration of the will of a majority of the voters or effective denial to a minority of voters of a fair chance to influence the political process.[74]

That is, "a major party ... would have to show that it 'had essentially been shut out of the political process.'"[75] Again, how exactly are plaintiffs to demonstrate such an effect?

At the time the *Bandemer* decision was issued, political scientists had just begun to establish quantitative measures of partisan bias in the relationship between votes and legislative seats.[76] The political scientist Bernard Grofman notes that, in its consideration of *Bandemer*, lower court judges relied on two different methods for assessing the fairness of a redistricting plan. The first seeks "to establish a baseline measure of (two-party) vote in the districts at issue using votes in some set of election contests that appropriately reflect underlying partisan support propensities (usually statewide ones)."[77] The second method "involves looking at a party aggregate share of the statewide (two-party) vote in the actual (type of) election contests that are under challenge."[78] The Supreme Court, in deciding *Bandemer* on the merits, did not identify a preferred method because it argued that evidence of a discriminatory effect must come from more than one election cycle.[79]

In the years following *Bandemer*, there was not a single successful challenge to a partisan gerrymander. Nevertheless, aggrieved parties continued to hold out hope that a redistricting plan would be so egregiously partisan that it would violate the Constitution. In 2004, plaintiffs in Pennsylvania thought they had just such a plan. The 2001 redistricting plan, created by Republicans, resulted in control of 63.2 percent of Pennsylvania's congressional seats (i.e., 12 of 19) by the GOP based on 60.3 percent of the statewide congressional vote. By 2004, Republicans were able to maintain their hold on 12 of 19 congressional seats while securing only 55.5 percent of the vote.[80]

That disparity was not enough evidence to overturn the plan, according to the Supreme Court's decision in *Vieth v. Jubelirer* (2004).[81] The majority's reasoning was that in the 18 years since *Bandemer*, no accepted standard for detecting partisan discrimination had been established. Indeed, among the four dissenters in *Vieth*, three different standards were offered. Lacking an accepted standard, four of the five justices in the majority argued that *Bandemer* should be overturned and that partisan gerrymandering was not justiciable. Justice Kennedy, the swing vote on the merits of the case, disagreed with overturning *Bandemer* and suggested that an acceptable standard might emerge in the future.[82]

One question that remained unresolved after *Vieth* was whether redistricting plans should be "evaluated at the level of the district or the [entire] plan."[83] While the plurality in *Bandemer* and Justice Breyer in his *Vieth* dissent favored evaluation of entire plans, Justices Stevens and Souter, in their *Vieth* dissents, preferred a district-based approach. Interestingly, as Daniel Lowenstein and his colleagues point out, "one-person, one-vote [i.e., malapportionment] cases are decided at the plan level while racial gerrymandering cases are decided at the district level."[84] Presumably, partisan gerrymandering is analogous to the latter, but this matter is far from settled.

Though it was still theoretically possible to draw an unconstitutional partisan gerrymander in the wake of *Vieth*, the main conclusion most analysts drew from the case was that it would be nearly impossible to provide evidence for the intent and effect of partisan discrimination, at least in the short run.[85] Until an agreed standard for assessing partisan redistricting plans was in place, those challenging such plans would almost certainly be unsuccessful.[86] Some suggested forcing the issue by working through state courts, from which an accepted standard might emerge.[87] Others argued for abandoning equal protection claims altogether and challenging partisan gerrymandering on First Amendment grounds. Gerrymandering, according to this argument, violates the free expression and political association rights of partisans who are disadvantaged by such plans.[88]

In 2006, the Supreme Court decided a Texas case (*LULAC v. Perry*) in which Democrats challenged a mid-decade redistricting plan.[89] A previous plan had been put in place by a federal judge when the Texas legislature and governor couldn't agree on a plan at the beginning of the decade. Because Texas Republicans used data in their 2003 revised plan that was relatively out of date (i.e., from 2000), Democrats argued, in part, that the revised plan violated the one-person, one-vote standard. They also argued that the process of mid-decade redistricting should be ruled invalid as it will always be motivated by partisanship.[90] The Court, once again divided in complicated ways, ruled against the Democrats.

Several dissenting justices in *LULAC* expressed interest in a standard, "partisan symmetry," that they thought had potential to garner consensus as an acceptable test of partisan bias in redistricting plans. The justices had been unaware of that standard during their consideration of *Vieth*. The concept of partisan symmetry, and its corresponding statistical methodology, is the product of years of academic research by several political scientists.[91] These scholars submitted an *amicus* brief in *LULAC* in which they explained that partisan symmetry

> requires that the electoral system treat similarly-situated political parties equally, so that each receives the same fraction of legislative seats for a particular vote percentage as the other party would receive if it had received the same percentage [of the vote]. In other words, it compares how both parties would fare hypothetically if they each (in turn) had received a given percentage of the vote. The difference in how parties would fare is the "partisan bias" of the election system.[92]

The scholars were quick to point out that symmetry does not require proportionality. In other words, it is not necessarily a sign of partisan bias if Republicans win 60 percent of the vote but only 45 percent of the seats in the legislature. All that is required to achieve partisan symmetry is that "the map treats similarly-situated parties equally – [that] both parties have the *opportunity* to capture the same amount of seats, if they receive a particular percentage of the statewide vote."[93]

Partisan symmetry would never be sufficient to establish that an unconstitutional partisan gerrymander has occurred. In his *LULAC* dissent, Justice Stevens refers to the measure as "a helpful (though certainly not talismanic) tool" and includes asymmetry as one of eight criteria for establishing a discriminatory effect of a partisan gerrymander.[94] Justice Kennedy also maintained that "asymmetry *alone* is not a reliable measure of unconstitutional partisanship."[95]

As it turns out, partisan symmetry wasn't the only measure competing for consideration as the accepted standard for judging partisan bias. The plaintiffs in a case originating in Wisconsin (eventually, *Gill v. Whitford*) relied heavily on the "efficiency gap."[96] This measure is based on the assumption that some number of votes in any electoral system are wasted. Wasted votes are those votes cast for a losing candidate as well as those cast for a winning candidate in excess of what is needed for that candidate to have won. A gerrymander is nothing more than "a district plan that results in one party wasting many more votes than its adversary."[97] The efficiency gap quantifies this as "the difference between the parties' respective wasted votes, divided by the total number of votes cast in the election."[98] The larger the resulting number, the more bias there is in the districting plan. That is, an efficiency gap of zero means there is no bias because each party is wasting the same number of votes.

The efficiency gap has been criticized on several grounds.[99] For example, urban districts tend to be overwhelmingly Democratic, not necessarily because of gerrymandering but because progressive voters tend to cluster in cities. Unfortunately, the efficiency gap can't differentiate between natural clustering and gerrymandering. In addition, the efficiency gap is premised on certain assumptions about the relationship between seats and votes that turn out to be problematic.[100]

Partisan symmetry and the efficiency gap aren't the only measures of partisan bias in districting plans. Scholars have suggested alternative approaches, such as the "median-mean comparison"[101] and a computational method that relies on tens of thousands of simulations.[102] Nevertheless, partisan symmetry and the efficiency gap are the leading contenders for a court-accepted standard by which to judge partisan gerrymandering. That is, they would be the leading contenders if the Supreme Court was interested in establishing such a standard.

Unfortunately for those who would like to see partisan gerrymandering outlawed, the Court has done a U-turn with respect to the justiciability of partisan gerrymandering cases. When the Court considered *Gill v. Whitford* in 2018, it remanded the case to a lower court based on concerns over standing (i.e., whether the plaintiffs were harmed by the districting plan in question and, therefore, justified in bringing the lawsuit). In the same year, the Court also remanded a North Carolina case, upheld a district court's denial of a preliminary injunction against a Maryland districting plan, and refused to hear a case challenging a court-ordered plan in Pennsylvania.

All of this seemed to be kicking the can down the road and, to some extent, it was (but not for long). In 2019, when the Court heard an appeal in the North Carolina case (*Rucho v. Common Cause*, in conjunction with the Maryland case of *Lamone et al. v. Benisek et al.*), Justice Kennedy had been replaced by Justice Kavanaugh. With Kennedy's openness to the possibility of an unconstitutional partisan gerrymander gone, the Court ruled in a 5–4 decision that partisan gerrymandering cases were not justiciable.[103] "Excessive partisanship in districting leads to results that reasonably seem unjust," wrote Justice Roberts for the majority.

> But the fact that such gerrymandering is "incompatible with democratic principles," . . . does not mean that the solution lies with the federal judiciary. We conclude that partisan gerrymandering claims present political questions beyond the reach of the federal courts. Federal judges have no license to reallocate political power between the two major political parties, with no plausible grant of authority in the Constitution, and no legal standards to limit and direct their decisions.[104]

In her dissent, Justice Kagan argued that "gerrymandering is, as so many Justices have emphasized before, anti-democratic in the most profound sense ... The practices challenged in these cases imperil our system of government. Part of the Court's role in that system is to defend its foundations. None is more important than free and fair elections."[105] Nevertheless, the upshot of the *Rucho* decision is that, for the time being, there will be no judicial relief from partisan gerrymandering.

The Court has made a neat separation between racial gerrymandering, which is unconstitutional, and partisan gerrymandering, which is constitutionally permissible. That distinction may not be as clear as it appears.[106] In states with significant populations of racial minorities, for instance, drawing district lines based on race and drawing them according to party may look very similar since voting patterns are increasingly linked to race. Indeed, to the extent that race can serve as a proxy for partisanship, as many conservative justices on the Court may be willing to countenance, we could soon find ourselves in a period of race-based vote dilution in the guise of partisan gerrymandering.

Conclusion

The reapportionment revolution of the 1960s forever changed the way legislative elections are held in the United States. As a result of the Supreme Court's decisions in the apportionment cases, state legislative districts within a state must now be roughly equal in size and a state's congressional districts must be strictly equal. It is now hard to imagine a time when political equality – "one person, one vote" – was not the prevailing standard in electoral democracy.

A series of Supreme Court cases, beginning in the 1980s, have dealt with the question of race and redistricting. Drawing district lines to dilute the voting power of racial minorities is very clearly prohibited, according to the Court. However, attempting to enhance that power by creating majority-minority districts could also run afoul of the law. Race, the Court has concluded, cannot be the "predominant" factor in drawing district lines. Indeed, for the time being at least, any use of race may be forbidden.

Partisanship, on the other hand, most certainly can motivate those in charge of redistricting. After more than 30 years of entertaining the possibility that a district plan could so egregiously disadvantage voters in one party as to constitute an unconstitutional partisan gerrymander, the Court slammed the door on such a possibility in 2019. A legal remedy to partisan gerrymandering now appears beyond reach.

Nevertheless, redistricting reform that constrains partisan gerrymandering is still possible. Options for such reform will be discussed in chapter 6. Before considering those options, however, we must understand exactly how gerrymandering operates and the effect it has on elections and American politics generally. The following chapter provides a gerrymandering "how to," while chapter 5 examines empirical studies of the impact of gerrymandering.

CHAPTER 4

How Gerrymandering Works

The previous chapter discussed ways in which the redistricting process is – and is not – constrained by constitutional provisions (e.g., equal population sizes and prohibitions on racial discrimination). Section 2 of the VRA reinforces the constitutional prohibition against discrimination based on race. However, there are a number of other standards or criteria that guide the redistricting process in the states. Most of these are encoded in state constitutions or statutes but some are simply widely accepted principles.

This chapter begins with a brief discussion of the agents responsible for redistricting. It then explores the criteria that are applied to the redistricting process. The bulk of the chapter explains how redistricting is done, including the data mapmakers use and the technological advances that allow them to move boundary lines with precision. Finally, the chapter will describe the techniques employed – namely, "packing" and "cracking" – to create gerrymandered districts.

Who is Responsible for Drawing the Maps?

In most states, plans containing district maps are handled like ordinary pieces of legislation. That is, the plans have to pass both chambers of the legislature (or the one chamber of Nebraska's unicameral legislature) and then receive the governor's signature. In some states, however, redistricting commissions have a role to play (though that role may be quite limited).

There are, essentially, three types of commissions: those with primary responsibility for redistricting; those that are merely advisory; and those that serve as a backup should the legislature fail to pass a redistricting plan. It should be noted that Iowa has a unique system for redistricting. There, a bipartisan advisory board provides guidance to the nonpartisan civil servants from the Legislative Services Agency who are responsible for drawing the maps. Once the maps are produced, they are taken up by the legislature and treated as a regular piece of legislation.[1]

A commission has primary responsibility for drawing congressional district boundaries in eight states currently (which might increase to nine if Montana is award a second seat in the House of Representatives following the 2020 census).[2] In another six states (or 14 in total), state legislative districts are drawn by a redistricting commission.[3] Membership on these commissions ranges from 3 (in Arkansas) to 18 (on the House Apportionment Commission in Missouri). Importantly, there is considerable variation in the independence of these commissions. Most are what might be called "politician commissions." These commissions, as Bruce Cain explains,

> are composed of elected officials or their designees. While they are not independent in the sense of being separated from the power and influence of elected officials, they are autonomous in the sense that they do not have to submit their plans to the legislature like advisory commissions or wait until there is a legislative breakdown like backup commissions.[4]

Some politician commissions are designed to achieve a level of partisan balance. These bipartisan commissions require membership from both the majority and the minority party in a state. Others allow designated officeholders (e.g., the governor or leaders of the state House and Senate) to appoint commission members. In these cases, the partisan balance on the commission reflects the partisan control of state government. If one party controls all branches of government, they'll have complete control of the redistricting commission; if party control is split, so too will be membership on the redistricting commission.

There is a subset of commissions with primary responsibility for redistricting that are free from the influence of elected officials. Currently, Arizona, California, Colorado, and Michigan use these "independent citizen commissions." The selection process for commission members differs in each of these states but the process starts with the creation of a pool of potential commission members from which the eventual membership is drawn. Details about how this works in each state will be provided in chapter 6. For now, the key fact about this model is that its "distinguishing features are the separation of the commissioners from elected officials and the ability to put district lines in place without legislative approval."[5]

Commissions without primary responsibility for drawing district lines exist in a handful of states. In six states, redistricting commissions serve an advisory role whereby the commission suggests a plan to the legislature, which can decide whether to adopt the plan. Some states use commissions as a backup. In five states, if the legislature cannot agree on a plan for state legislative districts, the commission will do so; in two states, a backup commission will draw congressional district lines if the legislature fails to do so. (In one other, Ohio, a backup commission is utilized for congressional districts if the legislature fails to pass a plan with three-fifths support and half the members of both major parties, in both legislative chambers.)

In about half the states, then, there is no commission of any sort. In those states, the legislature is responsible for drafting district plans, passing them, and sending them to the governor for approval or veto. Though partisanship is at least part of the process in most states, there are also well-established criteria that guide the process. It is to those criteria that we now turn our attention.

Redistricting Criteria

Recall from the previous chapter that the one person, one vote standard requires legislative districts to be equal in population size. Congressional districts within a state have to be strictly equal (i.e., as close to equal as possible); state legislative districts have to be substantially equal. Substantial equality has been taken to mean that the total deviation between the largest and the smallest legislative districts cannot exceed 10 percent of the average district population. This is simply a guideline and can be violated if there is a compelling reason for doing so. A few states limit total deviation by statute to something less than 10 percent and at least one (Iowa) takes the average deviation within districts into account.[6]

Recall, too, that states cannot discriminate on the basis of race and ethnicity. Indeed, Section 2 of the Voting Rights Act prohibits states from diluting the votes of minority voters or from making it difficult for them to "participate in the political process and to elect representatives of their choice." This would seem to encourage mapmakers to draw some districts in which a majority of the voters are racial and/or ethnic minorities (i.e., majority-minority, or minority opportunity, districts). However, the Supreme Court has also said that race cannot be the predominant factor in drawing district lines. As a result, "states must account for race in some ways, but may not do so 'too much.'"[7]

We saw in chapter 2 that the use of multimember districts
for congressional districts was banned in 1967. Most states
also use single-member districts for their state legislative seats,
though 10 states utilize multimember districts, at least partially, in at least one chamber.[8] Most often, these multimember
districts consist of just two representatives, though New
Hampshire has state House districts with as many as 11 members. Nevertheless, multimember districts are drawn according
to virtually all of the other criteria discussed in this section.

Beyond these three federal requirements – equal population size, no racial discrimination, and single-member districts
for Congress – there are a number of redistricting criteria
that states employ. In its decision in *Shaw v. Reno* (1993),
the Supreme Court made reference to "traditional districting principles." At that time, the Court recognized three such
principles – compactness, contiguity, and the preservation of
political subdivisions.[9] Compactness seems like a straightfor-
ward criterion. But what, exactly, does it mean for a district
to be compact and how would we know if a district was more
or less compact than another? Compactness concerns the distance between various parts of a district. A compact district
is one in which the various parts of a district are close to one
another; the closer all parts are to one another, the more compact the district is.

It turns out that there are multiple ways to measure compactness. By one count, there are more than 50 mathematical
formulas that can be used to determine a district's compactness.[10] Christopher Chambers and Alan Miller suggest that
compactness measures fall into three categories – those that
measure dispersion, perimeter, or bizarreness.[11] Attempts to
capture dispersion seek to "assess the extent to which a district is spread out over a large area."[12] These measures include
the ratio of the area of the district to the area of a minimum

bounding circle (i.e., the smallest circle that contains the entire district),[13] and a comparison of the length and width of a minimum bounding rectangle.[14] Perimeter approaches "use the length of the district boundaries as a proxy for compactness."[15] Typically, this is measured as either the ratio of the area of the district to the area of a circle whose circumference is equal to the district's perimeter,[16] or as the ratio of the perimeter of the district to the circumference of a circle with an area equal to the district's area.[17] Finally, measures of bizarreness "use the mathematical concept of convexity to describe nice districts."[18] We can think of convexity by imagining a rubber band placed around an object (in this case a district). The tighter the rubber band fits around the object, the more convex it is. District convexity can be measured as "the ratio of the area of the district to the area of the minimum bounding convex hull."[19]

The second traditional districting principle identified by the Court in *Shaw* is contiguity. This principle is quite simple. For a district to be contiguous, every part of the district must reside within a common border. In other words, there must be a single, unbroken, boundary around a given district. The only complication with this principle arises from the existence of waterways.[20] When water divides parts of a district, that district will usually be considered contiguous if a bridge crosses the water, connecting two parts of the district. To be contiguous, islands within a body of water should be located in the district of the closest mainland. Nevertheless, it is sometimes the case that "states use water as an excuse to fudge what it means for parts of the district to be 'connected.'"[21] That is, they use waterways as means of combining otherwise unconnected pieces of land into one district.

The preservation of political boundaries, such as cities and counties, is the third traditional districting principle. This is, perhaps, the oldest principle of redistricting. Before there was an equal population requirement, states routinely assigned representatives to entire cities and counties.[22] Today, the principle takes the following form in many states: "preserve counties when possible; if you must split a county, preserve townships; if you must split a township, preserve municipalities, then city wards, then individual voting precincts."[23] Smaller political units, then, serve as building blocks for larger districts.

There are many reasons for preserving political boundaries. Among them are the fact that city and county lines are taken to be neutral and that election administration is easier when multiple levels of voting districts overlap neatly. Ultimately, though, representation is the best justification for preserving political boundaries.[24] People who share geographical space, or live in what Nicholas Stephanopoulos refers to as "territorial communities," are likely to also share at least some political interests. Stephanopoulos argues that people have a subjective sense of connectedness to those near them as well as an objective commonality. As he puts it, "people who live nearby . . . may have similar income levels, educational backgrounds, or housing situations. They may work for the same local employer or industry . . . Or they may simply care about the effective governance of the place they call home."[25] To the extent that lower-level political boundaries are kept intact at higher levels, people with similar interests may be better represented.

Of course, it is also the case that there can be significant differences in the political interests of people who live near one another, just as people in different cities and counties can share vital interests. For this reason, some states require that "communities of interest" be protected in the redistricting process. According to constitutional law scholar Justin Levitt, "A community of interest is a group of people concentrated in a geographic area who share similar interests and priorities – whether social, cultural, ethnic, economic, religious, or political."[26]

Communities of interest present those drawing maps with several challenges. For example, it can be difficult to identify some communities of interest, particularly where social or cultural interests are concerned (as opposed to, say, ethnic or religious groups). In addition, how unique, and how large, does a community of interest have to be before it deserves protection? Finally, keeping a community of interest together may conflict with other redistricting standards such as preserving political boundaries or drawing compact districts.

Several other standards may also be utilized by states. In order to maintain continuity of representation, districts may be required to be as consistent as possible from one round of redistricting to the next. This is sometimes referred to as the preservation of district cores. Mapmakers may also be required, or at least encouraged, to avoid placing more than one incumbent in the same district.

Of course, district boundaries are always drawn with political goals in mind.[27] These goals, while political in one sense of the term, are not necessarily partisan in nature. Mapmakers may seek, for example, to enhance electoral competition in as many districts as possible. This is more likely to be the case when redistricting is handled by a non-partisan body or by citizens redistricting commissions. When legislators draw the lines, incumbent protection may be paramount. If partisan control of the process is split (e.g., a governor of one party and at least one legislative chamber under the control of the other party), so-called bi-partisan gerrymanders in which incumbents of both parties are protected may be the result. It is worth noting that the most blatant political goal of the redistricting process – partisan gerrymandering – is often in tension with incumbent protection. We'll consider each of the afore-mentioned goals later in this chapter.

How Redistricting is Done

Redistricting relies on population data from the US Census Bureau. By April 1 of the year following the constitutionally-mandated decennial census (e.g., April 1, 2021), the Census Bureau provides states with the population counts they need to create district maps.[28] (States with odd-year legislative elections will receive the data earlier in the year.) Additional data, including results from the American Community Survey (conducted by the Census Bureau every year) and political data like election returns and voter registration numbers, are also used in the redistricting process. States differ in terms of the data they use to supplement the population figures.

"Drawing electoral maps," according to Wendy Tam Cho and Yan Liu, "amounts to arranging a finite number of indivisible geographic units into a smaller number of larger areas. For simplicity, call the former 'units' and the latter 'districts.'"[29] The smallest unit of Census data is the census block, which consists of an average of roughly 100 people.[30] Census blocks are the foundation of larger groupings of people, whether as the Census Bureau defines them (e.g., block groups and census tracks) or as politicians view them (e.g., voting districts and minor civil divisions).[31]

Census data, while generally quite accurate, is not perfect. Unfortunately, some groups are "hard-to-count" because it may be difficult to locate, contact, or interview them or they may not be persuaded to participate in the census.[32] This results in an undercount of these groups. In the 2010 census, for example, American Indians on reservations were undercounted by an estimated 4.88 percent and African-Americans were under-counted by 2.07 percent.[33]

Given the systematic nature of census undercounts, the Clinton Administration had proposed the use of statistical sampling as part of the 2000 census. However, the Supreme Court ruled in 1999 that sampling cannot be used to appor-tion congressional representation.[34] It left open the possibility of using sampling in the redistricting process.

For the 2020 census, the Trump Administration wanted to include a question about a respondent's citizenship status. Opponents of including such a question on the census argued that it would further exacerbate the undercounting of certain groups, particularly those of Hispanic origin. In the summer of 2019, the Supreme Court upheld a lower court decision to remand the case to the Department of Commerce because the Department's original explanation of the need for the citi-zenship question was dubious. The Administration tried to claim that enforcement of the Voting Rights Act necessitated the gathering of citizenship information. However, the Court concluded that this explanation "appears to have been con-trived."[35] Indeed, there is considerable evidence to suggest that a partisan rationale lay behind the citizenship question.[36]

To the extent that such a rationale motivated the inclusion of the citizenship question on the census, it was an attempt to dissuade noncitizens (and perhaps even Hispanic citizens) from completing the census, thereby reducing their numbers in the population count. That undercount, in turn, would enlarge the size of districts in which noncitizens (and Hispanic citizens) live, which would dilute the political power of residents in those districts.[37]

An earlier attempt to force the use of citizen voting age population (or CVAP) in redistricting, as opposed to the cur-rent practice of using total population, failed in the Supreme

Court in 2016. In *Evenwel v. Abbott*, two registered voters in Texas sued to stop the use of a court-issued redistricting plan (based on total population) on the grounds that it violated the "one person, one vote" requirement. Though the districts were equal in total population size, they were considerably unequal in CVAP. Indeed, while the total population of the state senate districts in the contested map deviated by 8 percent, the deviation of eligible voter population was over 40 percent.[38] A unanimous Supreme Court ruled that states may use total population in drawing district lines. Left unanswered was whether states may also use CVAP.[39]

Though states begin preparing for redistricting well in advance of the receipt of their population data, the process starts in earnest once they have that data. In order to draw district boundaries, those drawing the maps rely on mapmaking software. This software is typically leased or purchased from a vendor, though some states, including Texas, have developed their own redistricting software.[40]

Scholars have recognized the potential for computer use in the redistricting process since at least the 1960s. Initially, computer-assisted redistricting was envisioned as a check against partisan gerrymandering.[41] Of course, computers also provided the capability to create more effective gerrymanders.

Redistricting software appears to have been used for the first time by those drawing district boundaries in three states in the 1971 round of redistricting and by three more in 1981.[42] According to a survey of redistricting authorities in all 50 states by Micah Altman, Karin Mac Donald, and Michael McDonald, by 1991 "all but four states – Idaho, New Hampshire, New Jersey, and Vermont – used a computerized system for their congressional or state legislative redistricting."[43] Altman and colleagues maintain that this explosion in the use of computers was due to the development in the 1980s of the first Geographic Information System software capable of on-screen line drawing. Still, the use of such software programs was "expensive because they required considerable computing power available only from mainframe computers or high-end workstations, and needed ongoing programming assistance and technical support."[44]

By the next round of redistricting, in 2001, computing power had grown tremendously and the cost of sophisticated software had fallen sharply. As a result, "redistricting computer systems were omnipresent, fast, almost 'shrink-wrapped,' relatively cheap, and standardized in their software capabilities."[45] The power and ubiquity of computing led many observers to conclude that gerrymandering had reached new levels of sophistication (and nefariousness) at the turn of the twenty-first century.

Altman and colleagues dispute this conclusion, at least partially. "Given the timing of its adoption," they write, "computing technology seems unlikely to be the primary culprit for changes in competitiveness."[46] They note, for instance, that responsiveness and bias in the estimated seats-to-votes curve for US House races "were clearly displaying worsening trends by the 1980s, before any substantial use of computers."[47] Similarly, "the dramatic changes in district appearance that has drawn so much attention in recent rounds of redistricting" precede the "widespread adoption of computing technology."[48] In particular, the compactness of districts had decreased and the deviation from "traditional boundaries" had increased by the 1980s (though the authors note that "a sharp increase in the number of districts with questionable contiguity" did occur as computer use in redistricting became prevalent).[49] In their analysis of the 1991 and 2001 redistricting cycles, Altman and colleagues "generally found no difference in district competitiveness and compactness across computer use in the states."[50]

This is not to say that technology has had no impact on the redistricting process. Altman and colleagues recognize that the speed with which maps can be produced has increased dramatically. Alternative boundaries can be created in minutes, rather than days, so those drafting redistricting plans can compare far more maps than they could in the past. In addition, the data sets mapmakers employ can be far richer, enabling a more fine-grained analysis of demographics and voting patterns.[51] This enables communities of interest, for example, to be better identified and maintained in potential redistricting plans.

Of course, these changes may also mean that the drawing of district lines for partisan advantage can be done more precisely. This is all the more possible, if not likely, given the extraordinary increase in computing power over the last two redistricting cycles (2001 and 2011). Indeed, Altman and colleagues acknowledge that "technology could be a contributing factor" to changes in district competitiveness and that some developments in redistricting software in 2001 "may foreshadow a change in how optimal gerrymandering can be achieved."[52] Though the influence of computer technology on gerrymandering may have been exaggerated in the past, there can be little doubt that technology has made gerrymandering easier, if not more effective.

Another way technology has changed the redistricting process is that it "has opened the door to electronic submissions of maps drawn by the public and by interest groups."[53] Interestingly, the public had some ability to participate in redistricting prior to the reapportionment revolution in the 1960s. The earliest effort by a public interest group to propose a redistricting plan, according to McDonald and Altman, was that of the Washington State League of Women Voters in 1954.[54] However, once the equal population requirement was established and the use of (expensive) computing systems became part of the process, the public was sidelined from the process. For roughly 40 years, from the 1970s through the early 2000s, the public and government reform groups had little ability to suggest alternative redistricting plans.

By the 2010 round of redistricting, thanks to several technological developments, the public was once again able to engage in the process. The first of these developments was the ability to run mapping applications online.[55] The increased speed of the Internet meant that the complex calculations that had to be made by redistricting software could be done "on a server that users access through their web browsers."[56] In addition, cloud computing made it possible to conduct complicated data processing without purchasing a powerful system for oneself.[57] Finally, open-source software now "enables developers to create complex mapping applications at a lower software development cost."[58] This means redistricting applications can be easily used on home computers.

Currently, there are two publicly available online redistricting applications. One is Dave's Redistricting App (now called DRA 2020 in its latest incarnation), originally created by Dave Bradlee. It can be found at http://davesredistricting.org (last accessed December 29, 2020). Perhaps the most widely used public redistricting application is DistrictBuilder, found at http://www.districtbuilder.org/ (last accessed December 29, 2020). Created as part of the Public Mapping Project by Michael McDonald and Micah Altman, this application has been used in numerous redistricting competitions.[59] These competitions act as a form of "public mapping advocacy" by organizations that press for redistricting reform (e.g., Draw the Lines PA).[60]

Given the power of computers nowadays, couldn't they just be programed to produce a fair – that is, non-gerrymandered – set of districts? This commonly heard suggestion was first made as far back as the early 1960s.[61] Nevertheless, it is a suggestion about which McDonald and Altman express quite a bit of skepticism.[62] Indeed, their conclusion that fully automated redistricting is not an alternative to gerrymandering was a large part of their motivation to create DistrictBuilder. Their goal was to empower human beings whose "complex brains have ways of seeing solutions to problems that might elude a machine."[63]

The most obvious problem with relying solely on computers to generate district maps is that humans would have to program the computers and that would require dozens of choices, many of which would be based on subjective assessments of what good representation means.[64] Furthermore, technical problems plague any attempt to have computers create districts that meet all legal requirements while also following traditional redistricting principles and being neutral with respect to partisan advantage. In a 1997 review of the potential for automated redistricting, Altman noted that the available methods for finding optimal districts using computers – the so-called "exact" and "heuristic" methods – were flawed.[65] More damning is the fact that the redistricting problem is "computationally intractable," meaning it is "practically impossible to solve exactly."[66] This is because redistricting poses a large and extraordinarily difficult mathematical problem. "For even a small number of census tracts and districts," writes Altman, "the number of possible districting arrangements is enormous."[67]

As a result of these complications, human beings will be the primary district mapmakers into the foreseeable future though they will, of course, rely heavily on computers in the process. Given the choices that have to be made by those drawing district boundaries, biases are likely to appear in most, if not all, redistricting plans. Some of these biases will be inadvertent and mostly inconsequential. Others, however, will most certainly be intentional and may have significant electoral consequences. We turn now to these intentionally biased maps, or gerrymanders, and the ways in which they are created. The next chapter takes up the question of how consequential gerrymandering really is.

How to Gerrymander Districts

When the actual line-drawing begins, those in charge of the process have choices to make. "Every set of lines," writes Justin Levitt, "has a predictable electoral impact."[68] One such impact is a high degree of partisan competition and mapmakers may seek to create as many competitive districts as possible. This is widely held to be a desirable goal but it is easier said than done.

Putting units, like precincts or wards, together to form competitive districts requires some amount of clairvoyance. How are those units likely to vote in future contests in the districts in which they are to be placed? The most practical way to answer that question is to look to past voting patterns. Essentially, the creation of competitive districts requires an estimation of what political scientists call the "normal vote," or "the expected partisan division of the vote in future elections for the office in question."[69] The normal vote can be derived in a few ways. As Bruce Cain, Karin Mac Donald, and Iris Hui note, mapmakers can use voter registration numbers (in states with party registration) or past election results.[70] Party registration seems to be an obvious proxy for the voting behavior of individuals. However, using it to create a normal vote measure assumes that people always vote according to their party registration. In a polarized era, that is a safer assumption than it would have been in past eras but it will nonetheless be routinely violated by many voters. In addition, partisan turnout differentials may have to be taken into account if voter registration is to be used to create competitive districts. A five-point Republican Party registration advantage in a given district may be less competitive than a ten-point Democratic advantage in another district if Democrats turn out to vote at much lower levels than Republicans.

If mapmakers are to use past election results to establish the normal vote in a given unit, they'll have to decide which contests to use. Statewide contests are preferable because the candidates and other aspects of the campaigns are held constant across units. Presidential races are often used but the high-profile nature of those races may result in more defection from normal voting patterns than we'd see in lower-profile statewide races. Cain and his colleagues suggest combining the results of six statewide races below the gubernatorial level for the previous two electoral cycles.[71]

Having decided which election results to use, those drawing district boundaries must decide what electoral margin should be considered "competitive." Ultimately, any margin they use will be arbitrary but it is standard practice in political science to consider anything within a ten-point margin to be competitive. A decision about what margin to consider competitive may be moot, however, since Cain and co-authors conclude, after "comparing the registration margins with the normal vote measure . . . and the Presidential vote . . . that party registration is generally a good on-average predictor of vote margin."[72]

More than a decade ago, the journalist Bill Bishop identified a phenomenon in the United States he called the "big sort." Increasingly, people were moving to areas in which they would be surrounded by people who were like them in virtually every way, including their political attitudes.[73] Given this reality, it can be difficult to place a roughly equal number of Democrats and Republicans in the same district, especially in relatively small districts like those for the state legislature. To grab partisan enclaves for inclusion in competitive districts, mapmakers may have to draw oddly shaped districts that reach out in various directions and over a considerable area. Thus, competitive districts are likely to violate compactness standards.

It is also important to keep in mind the distinction Michael McDonald draws between competitive elections and competitive districts. Though the two are certainly related, the factor that makes a district competitive – namely, partisan balance – is not the only factor that makes an election competitive. The level of competition in an election is also based on the presence (or absence) of an incumbent in the race, the quality of the non-incumbent candidates, and the amount of money spent by the candidates, among other factors.[74] Those responsible for drawing district boundaries may be able to create competitive districts but they cannot guarantee that elections held in those districts will possess the factors necessary for a competitive contest. Having said that, highly qualified candidates, with sufficient amounts of campaign resources, are more likely to be attracted to competitive districts than to uncompetitive ones, thus strengthening the connection between competitive districts and competitive elections.

Competitive districts can produce highly disproportionate seat-to-vote ratios. At the extreme, imagine a state with ten highly competitive congressional seats. If one party were to win all ten seats by a margin of 51 to 49 percent, they would have won 100 percent of the seats. In other words, the minority party, with nearly half of the vote (49 percent) throughout the state, would have no representation at all. Again, this is an extreme case. It may be more likely, given the closeness of the elections in these districts, that the outcomes would – almost randomly – result in a 5–5 split in partisan control of the seats. However, if the political conditions in the nation or the state favor one party even slightly, that party is likely to win a much larger share of seats than its statewide percentage of the vote would dictate. Furthermore, from election year to election year, shifts in the partisan advantage those conditions produce are likely to result in dramatic swings in party fortunes.[75]

When mapmakers deviate from drawing competitive districts, they often do so by producing a "bipartisan gerrymander." These occur when mapmakers from both parties cooperate to create districts that are safe for one party or the other. This is most likely to happen when control of the redistricting process is divided between the parties (e.g., the governor is of one party and the legislature is controlled by the other party).[76] Given the tendency, mentioned earlier, of people to sort themselves into areas with like-minded others, drawing safe districts shouldn't be difficult. Whether every single district can be safe for one or the other party is another matter but a truly bipartisan gerrymander could produce safe seats in the vast majority of districts.

When gerrymanders are bipartisan it is often an attempt to protect incumbents of both parties. Incumbent protection gerrymanders, as these are sometimes called, are a bit more complicated than simply drawing districts that are safe for one or the other party. As Levitt explains, for incumbents "not every like-minded voter will do: incumbents want most to keep the same voters with whom they have built up name recognition and goodwill over the years. Incumbent protection gerrymanders, then, tend to change existing districting lines as little as possible."[77]

Theoretically, bipartisan gerrymanders could create highly proportionate seat-to-vote ratios. In our hypothetical state with ten seats, assume the statewide percentage of the vote is closer to 60–40. It's not hard to imagine that a bipartisan gerrymander would produce six safe seats for the majority party and four for the minority party.

Of course, none of those seats would be competitive. This produces its own set of potential problems.[78] Voter participation may suffer as voters in both the majority and the minority in safe districts realize their votes are unimportant for the outcome of elections in the district. Theoretically, incumbents in safe districts may become unresponsive to constituents. Of course, the possibility of a primary challenge for an incumbent who steps out of line with district sentiment may be enough to keep the incumbent responsive. In fact, the opposite problem may occur. With the vast majority of their constituents on the same side of the partisan and ideological divide, incumbents in safe districts may become more extreme in their views. The claim here is that safe districts become echo chambers of sorts, where widespread agreement and encouragement of the correctness of the group's views amplify ideological perspectives. In this way, bipartisan gerrymanders are thought by many to contribute to political polarization. The next chapter considers the evidence for this empirical claim.

Incumbent protection notwithstanding, what we typically have in mind when we think about gerrymandering are efforts to give only one party an advantage in elections. Partisan gerrymanders are most likely to occur when elected officials are in charge of the redistricting process and when just one party has total control of that process. In such a circumstance, the party can draw boundaries as it wishes, as long as it stays within the legal constraints discussed earlier in this chapter.

There are several tactics partisans use to give themselves an electoral advantage. One of these tactics is called "cracking." In this approach, the line drawers take an area with a heavy concentration of opposition voters and, rather than keep them together in a single district in which they would have majority power, divides them into several districts where their voting strength is minimized. Theoretically, cracking could prevent the opposition party from winning any seats at all.

However, depending on how many districts have to be drawn and on how many opposition voters live in close proximity to one another, it might be impossible to crack those voters enough for the gerrymandering party to win all the seats. In these situations, mapmakers will often seek to minimize the number of seats the opposition wins by employing a tactic called "packing," in which as many opposition voters are placed into one district as possible. In this way, packing is the opposite of cracking.

Figures 4.1–4.4 illustrate how gerrymandering operates in a hypothetical state.[79] In figure 4.1, we see the distribution of voters in our hypothetical state. Figure 4.2 demonstrates gerrymandering by the Square Party. Notice how they have packed Circle voters into one district (#4), giving the Circle Party a 16–0 advantage in that district. To pack that district, the mapmakers have had to put voters in the northwestern part of the state with voters in the northern, eastern, and even southeastern

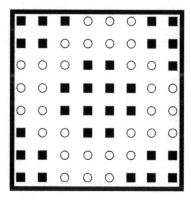

Figure 4.1. Distribution of Voters in a Hypothetical State

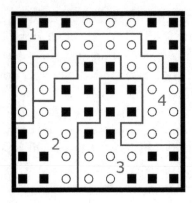

Figure 4.2. Square Party Gerrymander

Note: Districts 1, 2, and 3 are Square Party districts; they hold margins of 10-6, 11-5, and 11-5, respectively. District 4 is a Circle Party district, with a margin of 16-0.

regions of the state. The remaining districts are heavily populated with Square voters so the Square Party should be able to win three of the four districts quite comfortably.

In figure 4.3a, the Circle Party controls redistricting and they have cracked the Square stronghold in the middle of the state. That gives the Square Party a relatively safe seat in the southwestern part of the state (District 2) but gives the Circle Party an advantage in the other three districts. Notice that, given the distribution of voters in the state, the Circle Party can only give itself a slight edge in those districts. In an election year in which conditions favored the Square Party, the Circle Party might not be able to hold all three of those seats. As demonstrated in figure 4.3b, Circle Party mapmakers could create two safe districts for themselves by packing Square voters in a district (#1) in the central part of the state. However, the remaining district (#4) would be highly competitive (with a partisan split of 8 to 8).

Finally, figure 4.4 shows how a non-partisan redistricting

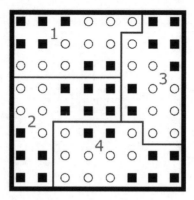

Figure 4.3a. Circle Party Gerrymander (Cracking)

Note: Districts 1, 3, and 4 are Circle Party districts; they each hold margins of 9-7. District 2 is a Square Party district, with a margin of 11-5.

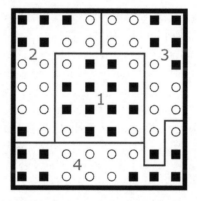

Figure 4.3b. Circle Party Gerrymander (Packing)

Note: Districts 2 and 3 are Circle Party districts; they each hold margins of 10-6. District 1 is a Square Party district, with a margin of 12-4. District 4 is a toss-up (8-8).

commission could create four highly competitive districts. To do so, however, the commission would have to crack the Square Party enclave in the middle of the state. If that group of voters was considered a community of interest, which ought to

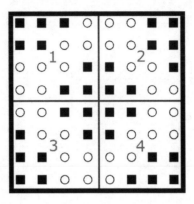

Figure 4.4. Non-Partisan Redistricting Commission

Note: All four districts are toss-ups (8-8).

be left intact, then the redistricting commission's map would look quite a bit like the Circle Party's packing of Square voters in figure 4.3b. Drawing neutral, competitive districts would be nearly impossible in this case despite the fact that there are equal numbers of Circle and Square voters in the state.

One last tactic used to give one party an advantage over another in a given district is called "tacking." Here, those drawing boundary lines reach out "from the bulk of a district to grab a distant area with specific desired (usually partisan) demographics."[80] By tacking additional voters from one party into an otherwise relatively balanced district, the party making the maps can give itself an electoral edge. Of course, voters tacked into a district have to be taken from another district, which may then create a competitive district elsewhere.

Indeed, to maximize the number of seats it holds, a party will often have to draw a number of fairly competitive districts. This, in turn, will make some of its incumbents vulnerable. While the trade-off between seat maximization and incumbent protection is real, it should not be exaggerated. As Anthony

McGann and colleagues note, "if a party is able to concentrate its opponents ruthlessly enough in packed districts (in which they win 80% of the vote or more), it can gain enough advantage to draw a large number of districts that are still relatively safe."[81] Both goals, therefore, may be met if those drawing the maps are resourceful enough.

Still, "relatively safe" may not be safe enough for most incumbents. As a result, there is often a tension among those drawing district boundaries even when redistricting is controlled by a single party. Incumbents are likely to want an incumbent protection map (i.e., a bipartisan gerrymander) while party leaders, seeking to maximize the number of seats they control, prefer a partisan gerrymander. It's a reminder that those drawing maps, whether partisan or not, have choices to make, and there is no redistricting plan that can simultaneously accomplish all the goals we may have for the process.

Conclusion

In most states, district boundaries are drawn by legislators and accepted (or rejected) by the governor, just like any other piece of legislation. To many critics of the current redistricting process, this seems like a conflict of interest. If elected officials get to draw the lines for the districts in which they'll compete, they're likely to create an electoral advantage for themselves in those districts. As such, reformers would like to see independent redistricting commissions in charge of drawing district boundaries. We'll explore such commissions in more detail in chapter 6.

Whoever is in charge of redistricting must observe certain standards that apply to the process. Districts must be equal in population (or nearly equal, in the case of state legislative districts) and must not discriminate by diluting the voting strength of racial minorities. Congressional districts must also be single-member districts. In addition, districts must be compact and contiguous, must preserve political subdivisions as much as possible, and should protect communities of interest, among other criteria that states may adopt.

The population data used for drawing maps comes from the decennial census, though data from other sources can be used to supplement census data. That data is processed by powerful computers, which have had an impact on the redistricting process. Though its effect, at least until recently, has probably been exaggerated by most commentators, computing technology has certainly made the job of those seeking to gerrymander districts easier. However, it has also allowed the public to participate in the redistricting process in ways that would have been impossible in the past.

Bipartisan gerrymanders, in which both parties agree to a map with districts that are safe for one or the other party, are fairly common, are more likely to occur when the responsibility for drawing maps is shared by the two parties, and are typically used to protect incumbents. Of course, public attention focuses mostly on partisan gerrymanders, in which one party controls the redistricting process and tries to maximize the number of districts it can win. To some extent, a party's ability to do this is limited by the residential patterns of the state's voters. Mapmakers can't move voters to different parts of the state. Nevertheless, by shifting the boundaries of electoral districts, they can group voters in ways that give those voters more, or less, ability to influence the outcome of elections.

There are two primary tactics for placing voters in electoral districts. Partisan mapmakers can "crack" an area with a heavy concentration of one party's voters into several districts or they can "pack" a district with as many opposition voters as possible. Cracking may prevent opposition voters from electing any of their preferred candidates, while packing concedes one district with overwhelming opposition strength but reduces the opposition's influence in all the surrounding districts.

This chapter illustrated these various techniques with figures depicting a hypothetical state with a given residential pattern. As these figures demonstrate, district maps for the same state can look very different depending on who is controlling the process. Having said that, the figures also demonstrate that, to some extent, mapmakers are constrained in what they can accomplish. In our hypothetical state, the Square Party can create three very safe districts for itself; the Circle Party doesn't have that luxury (though it can create three competitive districts that give it a slight advantage). Even a non-partisan redistricting commission has difficult choices to make. To create the most competitive districts, it has to engage in cracking. If it avoids doing so, it creates three lop-sided districts and only one competitive district. The point is simply that while gerrymandering can be effective, there are limits to its use. Indeed, we'll see in the next chapter that claims about the consequences of gerrymandering have often been hyperbolic.

CHAPTER 5

The Consequences of Gerrymandering

Political parties go to enormous lengths to win elections just prior to redistricting so that they, rather than their opponents, are the ones drawing district boundaries. For the 2020 election cycle, the Democratic Legislative Campaign Committee announced a $50 million effort, called "Flip Everything," to win state legislative chambers.[1] In addition, former President Barack Obama and former Attorney General Eric Holder formed the National Democratic Redistricting Committee (NDRC) to serve as "the first-ever strategic hub for a comprehensive redistricting strategy." That strategy would have four parts: "advancing legal action, mobilizing grassroots energy, supporting reforms, and winning targeted elections."[2] All of this was in response to the launch of the Republican State Leadership Committee's REDMAP 2020 campaign, which would "prioritize electing Republican legislators in states across the country in an effort to keep and expand Republican-controlled legislative chambers in advance of 2020 redistricting." They would do so with the help of "a $125 million investment goal."[3] In September of 2019, the initiative was relaunched as Right Lines 2020.[4] And, as an explicit response to the NDRC, the National Republican Redistricting Trust was created to serve as "the GOP's hub for coordinating a national redistricting strategy."[5]

Perhaps it's no surprise that parties would make such an effort to win elections. Winning elections, after all, is a party's primary reason for being. Nevertheless, extra effort, including the creation of organizations that have "redistricting strategies," seems to go into contesting elections leading into the redistricting cycle. This suggests that the parties believe that the ability to gerrymander districts will have significant consequences. Is there evidence that gerrymandering matters? In what ways might it matter?

This chapter examines the consequences of gerrymandering. The most obvious potential effect is on the ability of candidates and parties to compete for seats in the legislature or in Congress. Does gerrymandering actually result in less competitive elections? Does it enable one party to win more seats than it otherwise would have if districts weren't gerrymandered? To what extent does it contribute to the incumbency advantage? Gerrymandering may also influence voters either by affecting their likelihood to vote or their vote choice. Finally, gerrymandering is thought by many to exacerbate polarization by, for example, creating districts that are advantageous to more extreme candidates (whether in terms of partisanship or ideology). To what extent is this actually the case? There is considerable empirical research on these, and other, questions. What follows is a review of what we know about the effects of gerrymandering.

The Effect on Candidates and Parties

As has been noted several times throughout this book, gerrymandering is an attempt to give one party a competitive advantage by drawing electoral district lines that favor that party. Such an advantage, it is assumed, is artificial. In other words, gerrymandering is intended to give one party more seats than it would naturally get from the electorate if districts were drawn neutrally.

Of course, it's one thing to attempt to gain an advantage by gerrymandering districts and it's another to actually realize such an advantage. So, does gerrymandering work? That's a complicated empirical question that a number of scholars have nonetheless attempted to answer.

Before examining the scholarship, it is important to realize that the research on this topic explores the impact of redistricting, generally, and not gerrymandering *per se*. That's in part because it would be very difficult to establish valid criteria for distinguishing gerrymandered from non-gerrymandered districts without utilizing the outcome of elections held in those districts. There are, of course, measures of partisan bias that could serve as a measure of the degree to which districts are gerrymandered. (Some of these were discussed in chapter 3.) But those measures are based on election outcomes and, as such, can't then be used to explain election outcomes. Nevertheless, research in this area proceeds under the assumption that redistricting is a partisan endeavor and that those in control of the process will attempt to give their party as much of an advantage as possible.

The results of the research on the effect of redistricting on candidates and parties present a fairly mixed picture. Some evidence supports the view that redistricting has no influence on election outcomes at all; other evidence indicates a slight (perhaps conditional) impact; and a considerable amount of evidence leads one to conclude that redistricting is consequential. As a result, one could cherry-pick the research to support one's previously held beliefs about gerrymandering. However, a more accurate assessment of gerrymandering's effects must take the entirety of the research into account.

Competition
At the most basic level, gerrymandering is thought to alter the level of competition between parties. If it stacks the deck in

favor of one party or the other, we might expect it to reduce the number of competitive districts (i.e., those with a close division of Democratic and Republican voters as indicated by presidential election results in a district) or competitive elections (i.e., those decided within a narrow margin of victory, typically taken to be less than 10 percentage points). Edward Tufte's pioneering work on "the relationship between seats and votes" indicated that reapportionment after *Baker v. Carr* was responsible for the decline in competitive congressional districts between 1966 and 1970. Indeed, Tufte concluded more generally that "there is an immediate decline in the competitiveness of the races in the first election after the new districting."[6]

More recently, a series of studies by Michael McDonald and colleagues found that in both congressional and state legislative races, redistricting reduced the number of competitive districts.[7] However, others, like Alan Abramowitz, Brad Alexander, and Matthew Gunning, conclude that redistricting, at least in the three decades prior to the 2011 redistricting cycle, had "a negligible impact on the competitiveness of House districts" at the national level.[8] In a given state, however, Abramowitz and colleagues acknowledge that redistricting can reduce competition. Still, McDonald disputes their general conclusion and argues that their findings are "a consequence of measurement issues."[9] That is, "More valid measures of district competitiveness and redistricting institutions find that redistricting does have an effect on the number of competitive congressional districts."[10]

To the extent that redistricting hampers competition, Nicholas Stephanopoulos and Christopher Warshaw attribute it to "downstream effects" on political parties. In districts in which they are at a disadvantage, parties will find it harder to recruit good candidates, enlist numerous volunteers, raise sufficient amounts of money, and secure all of the other elements of a viable campaign. Indeed, as their analysis demonstrates,

"More severely skewed maps ... are linked to reduced candidate entry, poorer candidate quality, lower fundraising, and less support from the electorate [for the targeted party]."[11]

There is some evidence that redistricting actually *increases* district competitiveness.[12] Nicholas Goedert, for instance, found that in congressional elections from 1972 to 2010, partisan gerrymanders "suppress competition when the national electoral environment is closely balanced, but incite it when one party wins a substantial national majority."[13] This helps to explain what he calls a "pseudoparadox," which is that periods of heightened national competition seem to generate lower levels of local competition. According to Goedert, "partisan mapmakers will ... draw seats that will be largely safe for their own incumbents under neutral electoral conditions (when the national popular vote is close to even), but which will become increasingly competitive as national tides adverse to the gerrymandering party increase."[14] Bipartisan and nonpartisan districting are not as sensitive to the national electoral environment as partisan gerrymandering is.

In a study of state legislative elections in the first decade of the twenty-first century, Seth Masket, Jonathan Winburn, and Gerald Wright also found that competition increased when redistricting was handled by a state legislature with unified party control and decreased (as a result of incumbent protection) when the legislature was divided.[15] However, these effects were slight and did not last beyond the first election cycle after redistricting. An earlier study, by Marc Hetherington, Bruce Larson, and Suzanne Globetti, produced a similar result with respect to the dissipating effects of redistricting as time advances.[16] The authors found that quality challengers were more likely to run early in a redistricting cycle, which produced more, not less, competition in US House races. Nevertheless, they maintain that redistricting need not produce a great deal of competition. If mapmakers make incumbent protection their top priority, the result will be few competitive seats. However, the point of this article is that, *whatever* the baseline level of competition established by a new redistricting, districts will become decreasingly competitive as the cycle progresses.[17]

In his recent book, *Drawing the Lines*, Nicholas Seabrook found that partisan gerrymanders, generally, were not more likely than bipartisan gerrymanders to increase the probability of a US House seat changing control from one party to the other. However, when he separated Democratic and Republican gerrymanders in the analysis, he found that Republican gerrymanders (but not Democratic ones) were significantly more likely than bipartisan gerrymanders to improve the odds of a seat changing hands in the period from 1990 to 2010. The effect was relatively small "and only likely to be felt in the closest of House races" but, Seabrook notes, "when aggregated across all of the states where partisan gerrymandering occurs, is likely to produce a more responsive electoral environment."[18]

A number of scholars have attempted to determine the impact of redistricting commissions on competition. John Henderson, Brian Hamel, and Aaron Goldzimer compared redistricting plans drawn in five different ways (i.e., unified Democratic legislatures, unified Republican legislatures, divided legislatures or political commissions, courts, and independent commissions) to simulated alternative maps. Their results suggest that redistricting "marginally dampens electoral competitiveness as a whole," and, somewhat surprisingly, that "these effects are similar regardless of whether maps are drawn by (bi)partisan legislatures or independent commissions."[19] Similarly, Masket and colleagues found that redistricting conducted by commissions, whether bipartisan or partisan, reduced competition.[20]

This result led them to conclude that "taking redistricting out of the hands of a unified legislature and giving it to a bipartisan or judicial commission could result in less competitive elections."[21]

Of course, there is evidence supporting the opposite conclusion, that redistricting commissions produce more competition than partisan legislators. Jamie Carson and Michael Crespin showed that congressional elections in 1992 and 2002 were more competitive if they were held in districts drawn by redistricting commissions (or courts) than in those drawn solely by legislatures.[22] In a follow-up study that adds elections in 1972, 1982, and 2012, Carson, Crespin, and Ryan Williamson confirmed the earlier results. "If states wish to increase competition in their congressional districts," they wrote, "utilizing commissions (or courts) when redistricting is an option that should be considered."[23] Similarly, Eric Lindgren and Priscilla Southwell found that independent redistricting commissions and "backup" commissions produce significantly more competitive races than other redistricting methods.[24]

Goedert concluded that nonpartisan commissions create higher levels of competition than partisan or bipartisan redistricting. Unlike partisan gerrymandering, however, nonpartisan and bipartisan redistricting is relatively unaffected by the national electoral environment.[25] And Williamson, in a recent examination of redistricting plans and electoral competition, found that congressional elections "occurring under partisan redistricting plans witness lower levels of quality candidate emergence and higher levels of uncontested races than those taking place under court-drawn or commission-drawn maps."[26]

For Seabrook, the important distinction is between bipartisan plans and all others. In comparing partisan gerrymanders, independent commission redistricting, and judicial redistricting to bipartisan gerrymanders, he found that there was no difference between the approaches in terms of what he calls latent (or district) competitiveness, which is a measure of the normalized presidential vote.[27] However, partisan gerrymanders and redistricting by independent commissions and the judiciary significantly increase the electoral competitiveness (or the closeness of the margin of victory) of US House races when compared to bipartisan gerrymandering.[28] Thus, independent commissions, as well as partisan gerrymanders and judicially created maps, enhance competitiveness. Importantly, however, it is incumbent protection (i.e., bipartisan gerrymandering) and not partisan gerrymandering that hinders electoral competition.

Partisan Advantage

Gerrymandering is intended to help one party gain seats in Congress or in a state legislature. Thus, beyond the effect it might have on the number of competitive districts or elections, we would like to know whether parties in control of redistricting are actually able to gain an electoral advantage over their opponents. In one of the earliest studies of this question, Robert Erikson examined the influence of redistricting on the partisan distribution of northern seats in the US House of Representatives between 1952 and 1970.[29] Erikson notes that the "pre-1966 overrepresentation of northern Republicans in Congress resulted from a Republican 'gerrymander'": a pattern of marginally safe Republican seats and very safe Democratic seats."[30] However, this Republican advantage, which had mostly disappeared after 1964, was the result of voters' residency patterns and not the "deliberate partisan manipulation of district lines."[31]

More recent work on post-World War II congressional elections (from 1946 to 1970) by Gary Cox and Jonathan Katz modeled the effects of various redistricting schemes including partisan and bipartisan control of the process as well as "reversionary outcomes," which occurred when a legislature and governor failed to agree to a redistricting plan. Their analysis produced "strong evidence that both partisan control and reversionary outcomes systematically affect the nature of a redistricting plan and the subsequent elections held under it."[32] Cox and Katz also showed, contrary to Erikson's conclusion, "that the well-known disappearance circa 1966 of what had been a long-time pro-Republican bias of about 6 percent in non-southern congressional elections can be explained largely by the changing composition of northern districting plans."[33] That is, districting plans outside the south that had favored Republicans before the reapportionment revolution of the mid-1960s became bipartisan or pro-Democratic plans thereafter, eliminating the advantage Republicans had previously enjoyed.

Following Erikson by about a decade, Alan Abramowitz's study of the 1982 congressional elections found redistricting to have a positive effect on Democrats' electoral fortunes. The proportion of Democratic House seats relative to the increase in the Democratic share of the vote was greater in the 17 states where Democrats had complete control of redistricting than in other states. Other studies of the 1982 congressional elections also found a significant positive effect for redistricting.[34] As the authors of one of those studies concluded, "redistricting had a strong impact on the outcomes of the 1982 House elections," though they also acknowledged that the effect of redistricting was not as strong as the impact of campaign spending (on the part of the challenger).[35]

Abramowitz's analysis was applied to the 1971 round of redistricting by Richard Niemi and Laura Winsky. Their results for the 1972 congressional elections confirmed those of Abramowitz for 1982. "In both the 1970s and the 1980s," Niemi and Winsky write, "there is strong evidence that, on average, there is an initial partisan advantage for the party that controls all three branches of a state government."[36] However, this advantage disappears, gradually, over the course of the decade.

If some of the early work on redistricting found it to have a substantial impact on elections, other such work found more modest effects, if any at all. One study concluded that while states with unified control of government had relatively large partisan bias as a result of redistricting, there was no net national effect of redistricting in the 1982 congressional elections.[37] Similarly, an examination of districting plans from 1952 to 1982 found that "partisan control of redistricting does have the expected effect on seat outcomes, but only modestly."[38] Interestingly, the relationship between redistricting and seat gain had become weaker in the wake of the Supreme Court's imposition of the "one person, one vote" standard. Finally, a study of congressional redistricting in the 1970s found that redistricting preserved the status quo. Perhaps "a handful of seats" in the US House changed partisan hands in 1972 as a result of redistricting and incumbents were left "virtually untouched in their reelection chances."[39] Thus, there was only minimal evidence of successful partisan or bipartisan gerrymanders in the 1971 round of redistricting.

Studies of state legislative elections in the 1970s and 1980s confirmed the conclusion that redistricting had minimal effects and one widely cited study even found partisan fairness to be enhanced by the process of redrawing district lines. Howard Scarrow's case study of the 1971 redistricting plan for the Connecticut House of Representatives (which had been the basis for the Supreme Court case of *Gaffney v. Cummings*), found redistricting to be ineffective. The plan, which had been drawn up by a three-person panel consisting of a Republican, a Democrat, and a neutral member, was designed to achieve proportionality between votes and seats in the legislature. It failed to do so, however, because the panel "seems to have badly misjudged the firmness of Republican support."[40] Niemi's work with Simon Jackman on legislative races in the 1970s and 1980s found "no consistent evidence that relative seat gains in the election immediately after redistricting are related to who controls the districting."[41] With respect to partisan bias in election outcomes, they found "that moderate amounts of bias sometimes exist and that it generally favors the controlling party. Yet qualifiers such as 'sometimes' and 'generally' are essential."[42] And the conclusion from a study of 15 state legislative elections following the 1981 round of redistricting was that redistricting "can have an effect [on party winners] but that in most instances it does not."[43]

In one of the classic studies of gerrymandering, Andrew Gelman and Gary King examined elections to state legislative lower chambers from 1968 to 1988. They classified redistricting plans as controlled by Democrats, controlled by Republicans, or bipartisan. They then used a measure of partisan bias (i.e., deviation from partisan symmetry) as the dependent variable to see if redistricting plans produced more bias than no redistricting at all. The result was just the opposite. Elections held right after redistricting, regardless of who controlled the process, were *more fair* (i.e., were less biased) than elections held when no redistricting preceded them.[44] The reason, according to Gelman and King, "appears to be the role that redistricting has in shaking up the political system in combination with the many constraints on the mapmakers."[45] As the authors explain,

> if there is already a high level of bias, due to the previous decade's redistricting (or, more likely, to demographic and mobility

changes in the population over the decade), any political turmoil will have a higher probability of moving the system toward fairness since there is simply more room to move in that direction.[46]

Redistricting in the 1990s and early 2000s was becoming more sophisticated than it had been in previous decades. Yet scholarship that focused on this period reached no more definite conclusions about the consequences of redistricting. Niemi and Abramowitz collaborated on a study and found that, unlike in the 1970s and 1980s, "and contrary to the hypothesis that mapmakers are becoming more skilled at partisan line-drawing, initial results from the 1990s indicate that, on average, partisan control of state governments did little or nothing to enhance the partisan gains from redistricting."[47] John Swain and colleagues also examined the effects of the 1991 round of redistricting and, in doing so, asked two primary questions: "'Does a party benefit from redistricting?' and 'Do parties gerrymander?'"[48] Their answers were "that one party can benefit systematically from redistricting, yet at the same time [the] benefits from redistricting are not clearly linked to any obvious exercise of political influence."[49] In other words, redistricting in a given state may allow one party to benefit from the process, perhaps by "shaking things up" (à la Gelman and King), but that outcome would not be the direct result of purposeful manipulation of district lines.

In 1994, Democrats lost control of the US House of Representatives for the first time in 40 years when they lost 54 seats in the midterm elections of that year. At the time, some argued that the Democrats' defeat was due, in large part, to the creation of majority-minority districts. While Democratic candidates in those districts could win easily, Democratic incumbents in the surrounding districts, which had lost black voters to the majority-minority districts, became electorally vulnerable. Scholars John Petrocik and Scott Desposato acknowledge that majority-minority districts made it more difficult for Democrats in surrounding districts to win but their analysis led them to conclude that, in both 1992 and 1994, the loss of black constituents in those surrounding districts was not sufficient, in and of itself, to cost Democratic incumbents their seats. Instead, a surge of Republican support, particularly in 1994, was "*the* necessary ingredient in the Democratic losses."[50]

This example should serve as a reminder that those drawing district maps are, essentially, predicting how voters will behave in future elections. Since they're based on past voting behavior and on the assumption that partisanship is the primary driver of vote choice, those predictions are ordinarily quite accurate. Occasionally, however, the voters' behavior changes in response to a variety of factors. In a given election, for example, fewer – or more – voters of one party may turn out to vote than would normally be the case, or voters that typically support one party may decide to vote for the other party in one or more races. Thus, the best-laid gerrymandering plans can be spoiled by voters behaving in unpredictable ways.

An examination of data from the 1990 and 2000 redistricting cycles by Seabrook provides additional evidence for the limits of partisan gerrymandering. It is the case, as he shows, that control of a state's redistricting process enables a party to gain "an immediate and significant boost in terms of their number of seats in that state's congressional delegation."[51] However, any gains a party enjoys as a result of gerrymandering disappear fairly rapidly as marginal seats the party picked up following redistricting eventually flip back to the party that originally held those seats. As Seabrook summarizes, "Redistricting does not insulate a party's electoral majority in the face of popular sentiment, and the more seats a party attempts to gain through gerrymandering, the more it is likely to lose seats in subsequent elections where the popular vote shifts in the opposite direction."[52]

Indeed, aggressive gerrymanders, in which the party in control of redistricting creates a large number of very marginal districts in an attempt to gain as many seats as possible, can eventually backfire. When the political winds shift, the other party is likely to pick up many, perhaps even all, of those marginal seats, and the party that created the gerrymander could be left worse off than before the gerrymander. Such circumstances have been dubbed "dummymanders" by Grofman and Thomas Brunell.[53] Thus, while Nolan McCarty, Keith Poole, and Howard Rosenthal found that gerrymandering in 2001 helped Republicans gain an advantage in the House of Representatives in the 108th Congress (2003–2005), "the same gerrymanders may have been detrimental once the tide switched to the Democrats in 2006."[54]

In addition to the study by McCarty and his colleagues, there is evidence that redistricting in the early 2000s helped the party it was intended to help, at least in the short run. In their examination of redistricting plans from 2001 for the Texas state house, Brian Arbour and Seth McKee were able to estimate the effects of the plan that was ultimately enacted by the US District Court as well as two other partisan plans, one Republican and one Democratic. The enacted plan was a minor modification of the one proposed by Republicans. Arbour and McKee conclude that "the great variation in the number of Texas House seats that each party would have won is a function of the redistricting plan."[55] For Democrats, however, the edge that their plan would have given them would have been temporary as, in the long run, they would have become the minority party in the state house regardless of which plan was adopted.[56]

Texas was also the site of a great deal of controversy following the 2002 elections. In those elections, Republicans gained two congressional seats, bringing the party division in the Texas House delegation to 17 seats for the Democrats and 15 for Republicans. As a result of the 2002 elections, Republicans also took control of the Texas state legislature and the governorship. That development prompted Tom DeLay, the Majority Leader of the US House of Representatives at the time, to call for a new round of congressional redistricting in Texas. What would justify such an unusual mid-decade redistricting (unusual, at least, in modern times)? "I'm the majority leader," said DeLay, "and we want more seats."[57] In the spring of 2003, in response to the newly proposed Republican plan, a number of Democratic legislators left the state in order to prevent a quorum in the legislature. Nonetheless, the Republican plan was eventually adopted.[58]

McKee and colleagues compared the enacted plan to four other proposed plans to determine the effects of the five plans. "All five plans," they concluded, "show a Republican bias for both the short- and long-term scenarios, that is, *with* and *without* the incumbency effect, respectively."[59] The most beneficial plan for Republicans was the enacted plan and in the 2004 elections the GOP gained five seats in Congress (with a sixth additional seat picked up as the result of a party switch by a Democratic incumbent).

The most recent round of redistricting, as of this writing, was the 2011 round. As was the case for previous redistricting cycles, studies of the consequences of redistricting in 2011 have produced conflicting results. In studies of the 2012 and the 2014 congressional elections, Goedert finds some limitation on the impact of gerrymandering. In 2012, Democrats won more votes than Republicans, nationally, but fewer seats in the House of Representatives. Goedert's analyses of both state-by-state and aggregated election results in 2012 found that "while deliberate partisan gerrymandering produces additional seats for the districting party, partisan gerrymandering is not a sufficient explanation for the overall antimajoritarian outcome."[60] Instead, the high concentration of Democratic voters in urban areas, specifically in larger states (i.e., those with more than six congressional districts), is the likely cause of the pro-Republican bias found in 2012 (though a Republican incumbency advantage is also a plausible explanation).

In 2014, the pro-Republican bias of the 2012 elections largely disappeared. Because the electoral environment was very favorable to Republicans that year, the number of seats they captured was far more in line with the proportion of votes they received. Even the effect of urbanization declined in 2014 as Democrats won urban districts by narrower margins than they had in 2012. The difference in outcomes between 2012 and 2014 suggests that Republican gerrymanders in 2011 were designed to help the party under national electoral conditions that were highly competitive.[61] In a good Republican year, the advantages of gerrymandering dissipated. The difference between 2012 and 2014, then,

> highlights the importance of considering the national election environment, and its potential for wide variation, in evaluating gerrymanders and voting systems ... Partisan gerrymanders may be drawn to be most effective (and most biased) when the national electoral environment is close. But this same circumstance of a tied national election may also yield significant Republican bias due to geographic dispersion, making Democratic gerrymanders seem less effective and Republican maps more effective than they would have been under a different overall environment.[62]

If Goedert's work raises some doubts about the effectiveness of the 2011 round of redistricting, other research finds it to have been a very consequential round. Richard Engstrom identified seven states in which Republican-led redistricting produced a "manufactured majority" for Republicans in the House of Representatives following the 2012 elections.[63] Engstrom assumes this is the result of intentional gerrymandering, though he acknowledges that there are no standard criteria for classifying a state as having been gerrymandered. There are, of course, measures of partisan bias but such bias can exist inadvertently. Some would use disproportionality (i.e., a higher or lower percentage of seats won than the percentage of votes won) as a sign of gerrymandering, but single-member districts where a plurality of the vote determines the winner will virtually always produce disproportionality. Nevertheless, an extreme level of disproportionality (among other indicators) may well suggest that gerrymandering has occurred.

In four of the states Engstrom identified – Michigan, North Carolina, Pennsylvania, and Wisconsin – Republicans won a majority of the congressional seats without winning a majority of the vote in that state.[64] In all seven states, the Republican percentage of seats won was at least ten points higher than the percentage of votes garnered; in five of the states, this gap was at least 17 percentage points and in four of them (North Carolina, Pennsylvania, Virginia, and Ohio) it was 20 percentage points or higher. The election results based on the 2011 redistricting were remarkably consistent in the elections of 2012, 2014, and 2016. It was only the "wave election" of 2018 that served as what Engstrom calls a "gerrymander slayer."[65] Thus, according to Engstrom, the 2011 redistricting cycle would have shaped congressional elections until the next round of redistricting had it not been for an election that was unusually favorable to the party hurt by gerrymandering.

In their excellent book *Gerrymandering in America*, Anthony

McGann and colleagues argue that two conditions have to be met before we can say the opportunity to gerrymander exists. The first is that districting in the state is conducted by the state legislature and the second is that one party must control the entire process (i.e., it controls both chambers of the state legislature as well as the governorship). Even with the opportunity to do so, however, some states won't gerrymander congressional districts because the party in control dominates elections in the state so thoroughly that it doesn't need to gerrymander to win most, if not all, seats in the House of Representatives. Thus, McGann and colleagues suggest that only in those states where federal elections are competitive (i.e., the presidential election is decided by less than 25 percentage points) will the party in control of redistricting try to gerrymander congressional districts.[66]

In fact, with only a few exceptions, McGann and his colleagues found that states with statistically significant levels of partisan bias provide both the opportunity and the motivation for gerrymandering.[67] Furthermore, they concluded, "we can see that in the 2010 districting round, states districted for partisan advantage more aggressively than they did previously, even when we take into account who had political control of the districting."[68] Thus, regardless of the extent of gerrymandering in previous decades, there was far more of it in the 2011 round of redistricting. One very plausible reason for this development, according to McGann et al. is that the 2004 decision in *Vieth v. Jubelirer* sent a strong signal to state legislatures that partisan gerrymandering was legally acceptable.[69] McGann et al. acknowledge other possible explanations, but if *Vieth* did have this effect, one wonders what the 2021 round of redistricting will produce given the Court's 2019 decision in *Rucho v. Common Cause* that partisan gerrymandering is not justiciable.

Very few studies of the consequences of redistricting analyze more than one or two rounds of redistricting. One that does is Nicholas Stephanopoulos's examination of state legislative and congressional races from 1972 to 2014 and 2016, respectively.[70] Stephanopoulos sought to explain variation in states' efficiency gaps. As noted in chapter 3, the efficiency gap is a measure of the number of votes wasted by one party relative to those of the other party ("wasted" because they are votes in excess of what is needed to win or because they are cast for the losing candidate). When the efficiency gap is large, one party is more easily (or efficiently) converting votes into seats and, therefore, enjoys an electoral advantage in the state.

Stephanopoulos found that for both state legislative and congressional elections, unified control of redistricting significantly shifts the efficiency gap in the controlling party's direction.[71] Indeed, unified party control had the largest impact on the efficiency gap of all the factors Stephanopoulos included in his analysis. Interestingly, plans created by redistricting commissions do not appear to help one party or the other and had no statistically significant effect on the efficiency gap.[72]

The studies reviewed to this point are of high quality and undertake sophisticated analysis. However, one of the difficulties in assessing whether gerrymandering is successful is determining what the outcome of elections would have been in the absence of gerrymandering. Jowei Chen and his colleagues have addressed this challenge by using computer simulations to create a baseline of non-gerrymandered districts. "The benefit of using a computer to simulate districting," Chen and David Cottrell write, "is that it allows us to draw the same number of districts from the same complex geographic criteria for redistricting as the state boundary-makers themselves. The only distinction is that the computer is indifferent to partisan outcomes."[73] Comparing enacted district plans to the "simulated counterfactual," Chen and Cottrell find that "in most states gerrymandering has little to no effect on the partisan outcome of congressional elections."[74] In states where redistricting did have an effect, the impact is rather small. In fact, the net national effect of the 2011 round of redistricting appears to have been a gain of one US House seat for the Republicans.[75]

In an earlier study using simulated districts as a baseline, Chen and Jonathan Rodden found "that voter geography confounds the traditionally hypothesized relationship between gerrymandering and the partisan control of legislatures."[76] Specifically, Democrats are often at an electoral disadvantage because their voters tend to be clustered in urban areas. It is, therefore, patterns of residency rather than redistricting that contribute most to the pro-Republican bias in so many legislative elections in the United States.

Incumbency Advantage

Theoretically, incumbent protection (or "bipartisan") gerrymanders should aid incumbents in their re-election bids. If districts are drawn to be safe for an incumbent, that person should have little trouble winning. Of course, not all gerrymanders put incumbent protection ahead of other partisan goals, like winning a larger number of seats. As Bruce Cain explains,

> The key to a partisan plan . . . is increasing the efficiency of majority party strength, which will mean a redistribution of electoral strength for the purpose of maximizing the number of winnable seats. Some majority incumbents will get stronger and others weaker in inverse relation to their initial vulnerability.[77]

In the middle of the twentieth century, the number of "marginal" incumbents – or those with close re-election contests – began to drop and, for the next six decades, very few incumbents would be vulnerable to defeat.[78] Incumbency, in other words, provided an electoral advantage that nearly guaranteed success at the ballot box. Though many popular commentators assumed that increasingly sophisticated redistricting techniques were the cause of the incumbency advantage, most political scientists do not attribute enhanced incumbent safety to gerrymandering. Ansolabehere and Snyder note that growth in the incumbency advantage in the House and Senate from the 1940s to the 1990s was quite similar, even though seats in the latter are statewide and not subject to redistricting. Furthermore, governors enjoy a greater incumbency advantage than state legislators even though the former run statewide.[79]

Robert Erikson's analysis also raises doubts about the role of redistricting in the increasing incumbency advantage. Erikson provides the distribution of the vote for the Democratic presidential and Democratic open seat candidates in (northern) congressional districts from the 1950s through the 2000s. For 40 years beginning in the 1960s, the distribution of the presidential vote is unimodal, meaning that most districts clustered somewhere near the Democratic candidate's national share of the vote in a given year. During the entire time, the distribution of the vote in open seat races is also unimodal. But when the share of the vote received by Democratic House candidates in races with an incumbent running is plotted, one sees a bimodal distribution (until very recently). The different patterns of vote distribution for different kinds of races in the same districts suggest that bipartisan gerrymanders are not the reason for high levels of incumbent safety.[80] Furthermore, as Erikson points out, "the bimodality for incumbent-contested races is no more noticeable in the first years following redistricting (ending in 2) than in the final years of the decade, when any gerrymander effects would have faded."[81]

Several studies have shown that the redistricting method a state employs has little or no effect on the electoral chances of incumbents. According to Harry Basehart and John Comer, "If one simply compares the mean percentage of incumbents who win elections before and after redistricting in individual states, incumbents seem to gain regardless of the redistricting scheme."[82] In other words, bipartisan gerrymanders are no better for incumbents than any other method. Similarly, Henderson and colleagues find that redistricting makes the re-election of incumbents slightly more likely, "but these effects are similar regardless of whether maps are drawn by (bi)partisan legislatures or independent commissions."[83] Finally, James Cottrill finds that non-legislative approaches to redrawing congressional district boundaries (i.e., commissions) "contribute neither to decreased vote percentages when incumbents win elections nor to a greater probability of their defeat."[84] However, at least one type of commission – the advisory commission – may encourage higher-quality candidates to challenge congressional incumbents.

Despite these findings, there is quite a bit of evidence that redistricting hurts incumbents' re-election chances. As John Friedman and Richard Holden show, "changes in redistricting have actually *reduced* the success rate of incumbents quite steadily over the past century."[85] Like the work summarized in the previous paragraph, Friedman and Holden also find that the impact of redistricting is not affected by the mode of redistricting.

A series of studies, including several by M. V. Hood and Seth McKee, has demonstrated that incumbents perform much better in parts of a district they retain from the period prior to redistricting than in parts of a district that are new to them as a result of redistricting.[86] The reason for the difference appears to be that voters in the new part of a district are less familiar with the incumbent than are voters from the older part of the district.[87] As McKee has shown, voters with an incumbent who is new to them are less likely to identify that incumbent (through either recall or name recognition) than are voters who have already been in the incumbent's district.[88]

An alternative explanation for why incumbents are harmed by redistricting is that the process attracts stronger challengers.[89] To the extent that redistricting causes uncertainty, argue Antoine Yoshinaka and Chad Murphy, incumbents will be more likely to retire than to run in a district that is even partly new to them. Their results indicate that this is, indeed, what happens for "out-party" incumbents, or those from the party not in control of redistricting.[90] For those incumbents who stay and fight, the uncertainty of a substantial change to a district's population is more likely to induce a quality challenger to enter a race than will a largely unchanged district.[91] The upshot, according to Yoshinaka and Murphy, is that while redistricting may enhance democracy by creating more competition, it might also hinder representation by causing instability within districts, which interferes with the link between constituents and their representatives.

Desposato and Petrocik maintain that the incumbency advantage is variable and depends on the interaction of several factors. "When redistricting cuts [less partisan] voters loose from their old representative," they write, "their behavior depends on their underlying partisanship, the saliency of the election, and short-term political tides."[92] Their analysis shows that an incumbent's personal vote can be "as large as 15 points or none at all," depending on the other factors they identify.[93]

Though much of the research finds that redistricting is a threat to incumbents, some studies find the opposite. Tufte attributed at least some of the growing electoral security of members of Congress in the late 1960s to incumbents' "ability to exert significant control over the drawing of district boundaries."[94] Michael Lyons and Peter Galderisi examined the

1991 round of redistricting and found that US House incumbents fared better in 1992 under plans drawn by partisan, as opposed to nonpartisan, mapmakers and that they did especially well under bipartisan, rather than partisan, plans.[95] This is true for states in which reapportionment either adds seats or does not alter the number of seats the state has in the House. In states that lose seats, however, "redistricting is disruptive and threatening to incumbent security and in 1992 incumbent displacement was much higher than in [states that didn't lose seats]."[96] This leads Lyons and Galderisi to conclude that gerrymandering is "seriously constrained by seat loss" but is "more feasible" in states that don't lose seats to reapportionment.[97]

Finally, while acknowledging that constituents new to an incumbent's district are normally less supportive of the incumbent than are those who had previously resided in that incumbent's district, Richard Born finds some nuance in the behavior of new constituents. Generally speaking, new constituents are less likely than old constituents to be responsive to information about a district's partisan homogeneity and the incumbent's ideological extremity. In practice, that means that incumbents "with the most to gain from new constituents' non-responsiveness ... are those representing districts with the most unfavorable ratios of same party to opposition party constituents, and those with the most extreme ideology."[98] In other words, not all incumbents in new districts with constituents who don't know them (or the district) are equally disadvantaged. Some may even benefit, even if slightly, from the presence of new constituents in their districts.

As noted at the beginning of this section, the research on redistricting and its effect on candidates and parties is mixed. For example, there is as much work showing that redistricting makes elections more competitive as there is that it reduces competition (or has no effect whatsoever). With respect to the question of whether gerrymandering demonstrably helps one party over the other, the research is again mixed. Quite a bit finds that the party in control of redistricting benefits from the process but just as much finds no advantage for the redistricting party. However, a very close look at the results over time suggests that most research found redistricting to be relatively ineffective through the 1990s but that since then (i.e., in the 2001 and 2011 round of redistricting), a substantial amount of work concludes that it does create an advantage for the party drawing the maps. Finally, very little research on redistricting's contribution to the incumbency advantage finds that the process helps incumbents. A roughly equal number of studies find that redistricting hurts incumbents and that it has no effect on their electoral fortunes (and some finds the effect to be contingent on other factors). If the impact of redistricting on candidates and parties is unclear, perhaps we'll have a better sense of its effect on voters, the topic to which we now turn our attention.

The Effect on Voters

Voters may be influenced by redistricting in any number of ways. Much of the research on this topic concerns vote choice. That is, how are voters' decisions affected by being placed in one district rather than another? Before a voter makes a choice at the ballot box, however, they have to decide whether or not to vote. This section, then, begins with the influence of redistricting on voter turnout before considering the impact of redistricting on vote choice.

Voter Turnout
Some research on redistricting's influence on voter turnout, like that by Danny Hayes and Seth McKee, has found that the process has a negative effect among voters who are redrawn

into a new district. Less familiarity with their new representative raises information costs for these people and those costs
increase the likelihood that a potential voter will abstain.[99] In
a subsequent study Hayes and McKee once again found a negative turnout effect for redistricting. That effect was strongest
among Black voters, though it was mitigated when they were
redrawn into a district with a Black representative.[100]

Bernard Fraga also found that the race or ethnicity of a representative influences turnout in his or her district. "For African
Americans, Asian Americans, and whites," Fraga found, "reg-
istrants who are assigned to a district where their ethnic group
is a majority of the population, or where co-ethnics are on the
ballot, are more likely to participate in the subsequent election."[101] Curiously, however, there was "a slight decrease in
turnout for Latinos resulting from placement in a district with
a Latino incumbent ... and a substantial negative impact of
being assigned to a Latino-majority district."[102] The reasons
for this result are unclear and Fraga suggests more research is
needed to better understand it.

Charles Hunt found that, for the most part, redistricting's
impact on turnout is minimal. Voters who remain in the same
district as their previous representative are slightly more likely
to vote than those who are placed in new districts and, surprisingly, those who are moved to toss-up districts from safe
districts are less likely to vote (again slightly) than those for
whom district competitiveness did not change. Nevertheless,
Hunt showed that when party registration in a district changes
considerably, voters become quite a bit less likely to vote.[103]

Finally, at least one study concluded that redistricting has
no effect on turnout. Jonathan Winburn and Michael Wagner
examined voters in counties that were split into more than one
congressional district. Although voters in the part of a split
county with less district-county overlap are less likely to recall

the candidates for the House than those living in the part of the county with greater overlap, they are no less likely to vote.[104]

Vote Choice

Much of the work on redistricting and the incumbency advantage concerned the reaction of voters who had been placed in a district with a new representative. Quite clearly, voters are less likely to vote for an incumbent when they're new to a district than are voters who remain in a district with the representative they had before redistricting. As Hood and McKee have argued, redrawn constituents are simply less familiar with their new representative than are an incumbent's old constituents.[105] Furthermore, as McKee notes, "With the incumbency bond cut, redrawn voters are more responsive than same-incumbent voters to the prevailing short-term political climate."[106] Thus, when the political environment was beneficial to Republicans in the early 1990s, voters in districts that were new to them were more likely to vote Republican than were voters who remained in districts with their previous incumbent.

Even when the political tide rolled in the Democrats' favor, as it did in 2006, Hood and McKee found evidence that white voters in Georgia were more likely to vote Republican if, as a result of mid-decade redistricting in 2005, they had been placed in a district with an incumbent who was new to them than if they remained in a district with their old representative.[107] Essentially, Democratic incumbency had served to temporarily slow the realignment of white voters with the Republican Party. With the connection to a familiar representative severed, white voters in new districts were free to behave in a way that was more compatible with their underlying ideological and partisan inclinations.

However, it might also be the case that being drawn into a new district changes those underlying inclinations. Research by Mark Rush has shown that voting behavior is variable and partisan voting blocs are not particularly durable.[108] This is because "candidates of the same party are not fungible and . . . redistricting can change the context of an election (for the affected constituencies), as much as the retirement of an incumbent or the advent of an especially popular challenger."[109] As illustration of the latter point, Rush finds that when four Montana counties were moved from a Democratic district to a Republican district following redistricting in 1982, the new districts "became *indistinguishable* from the rest of the 'Republican' counties [in the Republican district] . . . despite the fact that they had been indistinguishable from the other, Democratic counties" in the previous Democratic district.[110] Thus, it appears that the partisan environment of a district can alter the voting behavior of those who are new to the district.

Of course, the influence of redistricting on vote choice is likely to be contingent on a number of circumstances. For example, while campaign spending has a similar effect on voters who are in old and new districts after redistricting, voters who are new to a district know less about the partisan makeup of the district and the ideological profile of the incumbent. As such, Born found that those factors are more likely to influence the vote choice of retained constituents than of new constituents.[111] The differing effects of these variables is instructive as they appear to "depend upon whether they emerge over the short-term period of the reelection campaign or are of longer duration."[112]

It should be noted that while redistricting appears to influence voters' decisions, it has more of an impact on the behavior of elite actors. Stephanopoulos and Warshaw found that voters are, indeed, less apt to support the party targeted by gerrymandering but that the effect is relatively small.[113] The larger effect is on the ability of political parties to recruit strong candidates and raise sufficient campaign funds. As they put it, "A party's appeal to the electorate is partly endogenous to how the lines are drawn – but it is mostly exogenous."[114]

Vote choice is affected by any number of factors (though, generally, party identification has the largest impact). By placing some voters in new circumstances, redistricting may well encourage new voting behavior in them. With respect to the likelihood of turning out to vote in the first place, redistricting does little to encourage it. At best, it has no effect on turnout though there is evidence that it serves to depress voter participation.

Polarization

One last consideration with respect to the consequences of redistricting has to do with the impact the process might have on partisan polarization. American politics, at least among elites if not within the citizenry, is undoubtedly more polarized now than it has been in over a century.[115] The question that concerns us in this section is whether gerrymandering is a cause of such polarization.

Polarization can be conceptualized in a number of ways.[116] For our purposes, the term simply means that the policy preferences of elected officials (and/or citizens, depending on the focus of study) are distributed bimodally along the left–right spectrum rather than unimodally, as in a bell curve. That is, polarization describes a situation wherein most elected officials are either on the left or on the right and very few, if any, are in the center (as moderates).[117] The level of polarization, then, is determined by the distance between the liberal mode (or peak) and the conservative mode.

The theory behind the claim that gerrymandering leads to polarization is that districts created to be safe for one party or the other will be represented by individuals who have no incentive to appeal to the ideological center or to voters who are not loyal partisans. Instead, these representatives have to ward off primary challenges from their ideological flanks. As a result, Democrats move further to the left as Republicans move further to the right, thus creating, and exacerbating, political polarization.

No one argues that redistricting is the sole, or perhaps even the primary, cause of polarization. There is, however, some evidence that redistricting contributes to polarization. Micah Altman and Michael McDonald maintain that the effect of redistricting on polarization occurs indirectly through a change in district partisanship.[118] Once the partisan makeup of a district is altered, the behavior of members of Congress should shift accordingly (at least in ways that are visible to their constituents). Indeed, representatives may anticipate district changes due to redistricting and alter their behavior even before new maps are adopted.[119] At any rate, Altman and McDonald document a "strong linear relationship between districts' partisanship and members' ideological voting patterns."[120] The greater the Republican presidential candidate's share of the vote in a district, the more conservative the member of Congress will be. This is true whether the representative is a Democrat or a Republican though, importantly, Altman and McDonald also demonstrate divergence in the voting patterns of Democrats and Republicans who represent similar districts in terms of partisanship. Since district partisanship is not a perfect predictor of a representative's voting patterns, some other factor or factors must be contributing to polarization.

Nonetheless, several other studies confirm that redistricting is a polarizing factor. In an analysis that linked congressional districts over time, from 1962 to 2002, Jamie Carson and colleagues found that "congressional districts that have significantly changed are having an effect on levels of polarization in the House, even when controlling for other prominent factors such as replacement [of incumbents] and electoral safety, which are often indirectly related to redistricting."[121] It should be noted, however, that the effect of redistricting in this study is rather modest.

Devin Caughey, Chris Tausanovitch, and Christopher Warshaw use the efficiency gap as an indication of partisan gerrymandering in a state and show that "an efficiency gap in the districting process affects the state legislature and the median ideology of members of the state legislature."[122] In addition, they find that state policy shifts in the direction of changes in the efficiency gap. State policy shifts significantly to the right as the efficiency gap becomes more pro-Republican and to the left as the gap becomes more pro-Democratic (though the effect is larger in the pro-Republican direction).[123] Stephanopoulos, who also relies upon the efficiency gap, finds something very similar for congressional delegations. "Moving from a gerrymander favoring one party to a gerrymander aiding its adversary," he concludes, "swings a delegation's ideological median by almost a full standard deviation – all without changing the mind of a single voter."[124]

Studies by Matthew Hayes and colleagues and by Michael Crespin show that changes in districts due to redistricting influence the behavior of members of Congress. Hayes and colleagues find that representatives alter their agendas (i.e., legislative priorities) in response to changing district demographics and their roll-call voting in response to shifts in partisan makeup of their districts.[125] Crespin's results, while not necessarily contradicting those of Hayes et al., are somewhat different. According to Crespin, representatives are responsive to changes in their districts with respect to votes they cast that are visible to their constituents (i.e., on "final passage" of legislation) but not to procedural votes, which are important to a representative's party.[126]

Finally, in his book *Party Polarization in Congress*, Sean Theriault tests a number of claims about redistricting and its effect on polarization. He summarizes the results as follows:

> Statistically significant findings show that new districts are more polarized than old districts . . ., new congressional lines yield more polarized voting patterns than old congressional lines . . ., states that purposefully partisan redistrict yield more polarized districts and representatives than states that do not . . ., and congresses with newly redistricted members in the House polarize above and beyond the Senate.[127]

Ultimately, though, Theriault concludes that no more than 20 percent of the polarization in the House between the early 1970s and the early 2000s is attributable to redistricting.[128]

Not all political scientists are convinced that redistricting contributes to polarization. In his primer on polarization, Nolan McCarty discusses several reasons to doubt that redistricting is to blame. One problem with the argument that redistricting causes polarization is that it assumes that gerrymandering produces safe districts. As McCarty notes, however, partisan gerrymandering produces "a small number of very partisan districts controlled by the minority party and a larger number of somewhat less partisan districts that lean toward the majority party."[129] Only bipartisan (incumbent protection) gerrymanders produce mostly safe districts and polarization makes these types of gerrymanders less likely because they require a certain level of compromise that is difficult to achieve in a polarized environment. Furthermore, polarization does not seem to increase more in elections that follow redistricting than at other times.[130]

A third reason McCarty offers is based on research he conducted with Keith Poole and Howard Rosenthal. McCarty notes that polarization can take two forms – sorting and divergence. Sorting occurs when liberal Democrats represent liberal districts and conservative Republicans represent conservative districts. Divergence "occurs when Democratic and Republican legislators represent otherwise identical districts in increasingly extreme ways."[131] For McCarty, the claim that gerrymandering causes polarization is a claim that polarization is caused by sorting because gerrymandering allegedly creates extreme (i.e., safe) districts represented by extreme legislators rather than relatively competitive districts represented by extreme legislators. However, in his study with Poole and Rosenthal, divergence, not sorting, accounted for the vast majority of the polarization observed.[132]

A final reason to doubt that gerrymandering is a primary cause of polarization, according to McCarty, is also based on his work with Poole and Rosenthal. McCarty and colleagues simulated redistricting procedures to determined expected levels of polarization in randomly created districts. "The difference between the actual polarization and these simulated procedures," they write, "allows us to establish estimates of the upper bound of the gerrymandering effect."[133] At most, they find, gerrymandering is responsible for "10–15% of the increase in polarization since the 1970s" and, interestingly, that "upper bound does not increase substantially following redistricting as the gerrymandering hypothesis would suggest."[134]

McCarty is not the only scholar to question the impact of gerrymandering on polarization. Alan Abramowitz has noted that members of Congress from marginal districts are as extreme as those from safe districts. In addition, the Senate has polarized almost as much as the House has and, of course, the Senate is not subject to redistricting.[135] A common response to this claim about the Senate is that polarization in the upper chamber is likely the result of members of the House moving to the Senate. Thus, polarization caused by the gerrymandering of House districts is carried into the Senate. However, Thomas Mann notes the "striking similarity in the timing and shape of the rise of polarization in the two bodies."[136] That is, polarizing in the House and Senate occurred simultaneously.

Mann's own analysis concludes that gerrymandering is not a cause of polarization in the House. Like Abramowitz, Mann shows that a candidate's margin of victory (i.e., how safe they are) is unrelated to the ideological extremity of his or her voting record in Congress.[137] That is, a representative is as likely to be very liberal (or very conservative) in a competitive district as in a district drawn to be safe for his or her party. Interestingly, Mann suggests that gerrymandering is more a consequence of polarization than a cause of it. When the stakes of every election cycle are as high as they are in the current environment, the political parties "have a strong incentive to manipulate the playing field and rules of the game to boost their party's prospects of holding or gaining majority control."[138]

Masket, Winburn, and Wright examined polarization in state legislatures and found that, between 1999 and 2004, polarization declined in states in which either the legislature or a partisan commission drew district lines; in states using nonpartisan commissions or in which courts created the maps, polarization actually increased.[139] Based on this result, the authors conclude that "partisan redistricting schemes are, if anything, associated with declining legislative polarization."[140] In order to expand the period of time under review, Masket and colleagues examined California State Assembly districts from 1976 to 2004. The measure of polarization in this case is not based on representatives' ideological vote scores but on the partisan voting patterns of district residents. As the partisan divide between districts represented by Democrats and those represented by Republicans increases (i.e., as districts polarize), members of the State Assembly are increasingly safe in their seats. Over time, district polarization increases quite dramatically and, still, "the increased electoral safety that occurs *between* redistrictings is greater than that which occurs *during* them."[141]

What conclusions can we draw about the contribution of gerrymandering to polarization? Not unlike most of the empirical questions addressed in this chapter, the evidence on polarization is mixed. There is good reason, and quite a bit of evidence, to conclude that gerrymandering is not responsible for polarization. There is also plenty of evidence suggesting that it plays a role. To the extent that it does, however, that role is a relatively minor one.

Conclusion

In this chapter we've attempted to identify the consequences of redistricting and gerrymandering. Unfortunately, we're left with an unclear picture. There is evidence that redistricting both enhances and hinders competitive elections; that it gives the party controlling the process an advantage and that it doesn't; that it hurts incumbents' re-election efforts and that it either has no effect or helps incumbents; that it depresses turnout and that it has no effect; and that it contributes to polarization and that it doesn't.

Redistricting does appear to affect vote choice by placing some voters in new districts, which, in turn, alters their previous behavior. This is probably not good news for incumbents because voters new to their districts are less familiar with them and are, therefore, less likely to vote for them. In some circumstances, voters in new districts rely more heavily on their partisanship than they had previously and in other circumstances the pattern of their voting shifts to match the partisan leanings of the older parts of the district.

That there is mixed evidence of the effects of redistricting and gerrymandering should not be surprising. The complexity of social science research on any topic often leads to nuanced, if not muddled, results, particularly when taken as a whole. This is the result of countless decisions empirical scholars have to make when they attempt to measure some aspect of human behavior.

We could choose to believe the evidence of gerrymandering's malicious effects and ignore evidence to the contrary; or we could do the opposite, and put stock in the evidence that gerrymandering is ineffectual and ignore evidence that suggests it does harm. Perhaps the most reasonable conclusion to reach is that while gerrymandering may not be as pernicious as it is often portrayed, neither is it entirely innocent. As such, it is worth giving serious thought to how redistricting can be reformed to reduce the likelihood – or the public perception – that it damages fair elections. It's to the consideration of redistricting reform options that we turn in the following chapter.

CHAPTER 6

Reform Proposals

This book has introduced the process of redistricting and its controversial variant, gerrymandering. I've traced the history of gerrymandering; reviewed the constitutional constraints on redistricting and the current legal status of gerrymandering; described how redistricting, generally, and gerrymandering, specifically, are conducted; and examined the consequences of redistricting and gerrymandering. In this chapter, I explore proposals to reform the process.

The research on redistricting, as we've seen, is mixed with respect to the impact redistricting and gerrymandering may have on elections and representation. While we can't be certain as to the degree, and even the direction, of its effects, it is safe to assume that while gerrymandering does influence the American political system, its influence is nowhere near as powerful as many critics would suggest.

Of course, there are good reasons to reform the redistricting process even if its effects are minimal. As Thomas Mann has argued, "Gerrymandering merits our continued attention if only because it reinforces developments set in motion by other forces, operates at the margin to decrease competition, and fuels further polarization."[1] I would add that, warranted or not, the widespread dissatisfaction with gerrymandering that we documented in chapter 1 compels us to give serious consideration to reform. When a democratic citizenry is as opposed to a political process as the American public is to gerrymandering, the legitimacy of the electoral system is threatened. This does not, of course, mean that simply because the American public dislikes an aspect of the political system, we must eliminate or replace it. Some aspects of the system are necessary for a healthy democracy even if the public doesn't realize it. Political parties, for instance, are essential for mass democracy to operate and yet the public sees them as the root of a great deal of evil in the system.

Indeed, there is a reasonable argument for maintaining the redistricting process as it currently operates. We described the "realpolitik" view of redistricting in chapter 1 so, for brevity's sake, I will only briefly summarize it here. It argues, simply, that no system is perfect and that all systems will be shot through with politics.[2] To try to take politics out of the process by turning it over to a supposedly apolitical body is itself a political choice, and it could be one that hinders the operation of democracy by making it hard to hold those who draw district lines accountable. In addition, some potential reforms could weaken representation by, for example, reducing the number of constituents who are represented by someone who shares their political preferences.[3]

Nevertheless, we'll proceed as though reform of the redistricting process is necessary, if for no other reason than to restore some faith in legislative elections in the United States. The public should be able to trust that election outcomes are not, essentially, determined in advance. If instead, they believe that their choices in the voting booth are meaningless because the outcome of state legislative and US House races is preordained, they are likely to stop voting. That would pose its own threat to the political system and would contribute to the illegitimacy of American elections. The only way to credibly claim to the public that the system is not rigged – that politicians, that is, are not selecting their voters before the voters elect the politicians – is to remove the process from control by state legislatures.

We'll begin our review of reform options with the least radical departure from the usual process and continue through to the most radical break from the status quo. Specifically, we'll start by looking at models of bureaucratic redistricting, one of which keeps the state legislature as the ultimate decision-making body. We'll then move to redistricting commissions. These come in several varieties, from those consisting of appointed politicians to those made up entirely of citizens, some of whom may even be selected randomly from a pool of applicants. Finally, we'll explore the use of multimember districts, which, in the most dramatic break from the status quo, would use proportional election rules to elect representatives.

In recent years, reform measures on the ballot in several states have been supported by clear majorities of the voters. As such, this seems an opportune moment to change the way we draw district boundaries, if we so choose. Whether reform efforts will be successful and, if so, what form the change would take is obviously unknown at the moment. Nevertheless, this chapter provides a range of options for those looking to initiate such change.

Bureaucratic Redistricting – The "Iowa Model" and Missouri's (Short-Lived) State Demographer

There are two redistricting models that rely heavily on bureaucratic expertise to at least initiate the process. In Iowa, civil servants in the Legislative Services Agency (LSA) are responsible for drawing congressional and state legislative district maps.[4] To assist them in their duties, a Temporary Redistricting Advisory Commission is formed, to which the majority and minority leaders in the State House and Senate each appoint one member. The four appointees then select a fifth member, who will serve as chairperson. The advisory commission answers questions from the LSA about redistricting requirements that are not clearly addressed by state or federal law; establishes policies for the sharing of information about redistricting plans with individuals outside the LSA; and, once a bill containing the redistricting plans has been presented to the state legislature, holds three public hearings about those plans and issues a report to the legislature on the comments gathered at those hearings.[5]

Once the LSA submits redistricting bills to the General Assembly, legislators must vote them up or down. (Amendments are only permitted to correct factual errors in the bills.) If they reject an initial redistricting plan, the LSA has 35 days to submit a new plan. If the General Assembly rejects the second plan, a third plan is submitted, though this plan can be amended in any way, for any reason. At this point, the General Assembly may also choose to produce its own map. If no state legislative plan is adopted by September 1, the Iowa Supreme Court is charged with creating a plan. Furthermore, the Court automatically reviews any redistricting plan that is drafted by the legislature.[6]

This approach was first employed in Iowa in the 1981 round of redistricting. Interestingly, the General Assembly has never drawn a plan on its own, nor has it ever amended a plan. It did, however, take the submission of a third iteration before legislators accepted the LSA's plan in 1981.[7]

One of the aspects of the Iowa model that is most attractive to reformers is the fact that the LSA is prohibited from using "political data" as they draw district boundaries. For the purposes of redistricting in Iowa, "political data" includes addresses of incumbents, the political affiliations of voters, previous election results, and demographic information "other than population head counts, except as required by the Constitution and the laws of the United States."[8] This prohibition is intended to help achieve the following goal, as stipulated by Iowa law: "No district shall be drawn for the purpose of favoring a political party, incumbent legislator or member of Congress, or other person or group."[9]

In 2018, Missouri voters approved Constitutional Amendment 1 with 62 percent of the vote. Among changes to lobbying and campaign finance in the state, Amendment 1 established a new system of redistricting for state legislative districts. Missouri had previously relied on redistricting commissions to redraw State House and Senate districts. For the House Apportionment Commission, the two party committees in each of the state's eight congressional districts nominated two individuals and the governor would select one person from each party in each congressional district for a total of 16 members. The state party committees nominated ten individuals each for the Senate Apportionment Commission and the governor would pick five individuals from each party for a total of ten commissioners.[10]

The two legislative commissions were to remain in use following Amendment 1. However, a non-partisan state demographer was to draw and submit district plans to the commissions for their consideration. Once applications for the position of state demographer had been received, the state auditor was to send the majority and minority leaders of the Senate a list of at least three qualified applicants. The Senate leaders would then select one of them to be the demographer. In the event that the leaders could not agree, each could strike up to one-third of the list of qualified applicants and the state auditor would choose one of the remaining applicants at random.[11]

Once the demographer had drawn new State House and Senate districts, the tentative plans were to be submitted to the redistricting commissions. A commission could amend a plan provided any changes had the support of 70 percent of the commissioners. If no changes were made or approved, the demographer's tentative plans were to have been adopted.[12]

In 2020, Missouri voters were asked to reconsider the redistricting reforms they had passed in 2018. By a margin of 51 to 49 percent, voters chose to eliminate the position of state demographer and to increase membership on each of the redistricting commissions to 20 (consisting of an equal number of Republicans and Democrats). Though the state demographer model was never implemented in Missouri, it nevertheless serves as a reform proposal that other states might consider.

The redistricting process in Iowa and Missouri's would-be state demographer model both rely on experts to propose initial plans. Where they differ is that Iowa's legislature has the final say on the adoption of redistricting plans and legislators may be able to draft their own plan. In Missouri, both under the state demographer model and as the process was revised in 2020, the ultimate decision resides with independent redistricting commissions. Thus, the Iowa model is only a minor variation on the status quo, whereas the Missouri approach is a more significant change to the way redistricting is typically done (and currently belongs to a category of reform we'll explore in the following section). If relying on a small group of non-partisan bureaucrats, or even a single expert, to draw district boundaries sounds like a good idea, what if we could rely on a computer to generate maps? Reformers have long suggested that algorithms could be used to produce neutral redistricting plans. In perhaps the earliest call for automated redistricting, William Vickrey maintained,

> elimination of gerrymandering would seem to require the establishment of an automatic and impersonal procedure for

> carrying out a redistricting. It appears to be not at all difficult to devise rules for doing this which will produce results not markedly inferior to those which would be arrived at by a genuinely disinterested commission.[13]

Following on the heels of Vickrey's argument, Stuart Nagel developed a software program "to implement the value judgments of those responsible for reapportionment. Not only can it transfer a set of agreed-upon values into a concrete plan, it can also provide alternative redistricting plans predicated on conflicting values and thereby facilitate compromise."[14]

Of course, computer-generated redistricting plans would not eliminate the role of human beings in the process. We might, for instance, need the assistance of computer scientists, though as we discussed in chapter 4 (and will consider further in the following section), the widespread availability and ease of use of computers and mapmaking software make it possible nowadays for nearly anyone to create district maps. The more indispensable human role in automated redistricting, as Nagel suggests, is determining what set of values or priorities the algorithm will reflect.

As it turns out, redistricting presents a kind of computing problem that cannot be solved, or at least not solved in a reasonable amount of time.[15] A technical understanding of the problem (called an "NP-hard problem") is beyond the scope of this book. For our purposes, the point is simply that "the problem of finding an optimal districting plan is computationally complex; any attempt will most likely be thwarted by the size and complexity of the redistricting problem."[16] What we mean by the "optimal districting plan" is simply the one that best satisfies all the criteria provided for in the algorithm.[17] One might seek, for example, the most "compact, contiguous, equal-population districts."[18] However, Richard Kueng and colleagues have shown that "even for simple definitions of

'fair' and 'legal,' deciding whether there exists a fair redistricting among legal maps is NP-hard."[19]

One problem with automated redistricting, then, is simply
computational. As Micah Altman and Michael McDonald
explain, an optimal redistricting plan may take contemporary
computers billions of years to produce.[20] However, Altman and
McDonald also identify a second problem, which is that "there
is a large gap between identifying representational values and
creating criteria reflecting those values that can be optimized in
a computer."[21] Even if we were to agree that districts must be
"fair" to all parties, what instructions or specifications do we
put into our algorithm to produce fairness? The same can be
said of any redistricting criteria, including compactness, contiguity, etc. Thus, even if we wanted to let computers generate
ideal districts based on an agreed upon set of criteria, we're not
likely to be able to do so (at least at the moment).

Independent Redistricting Commissions and Public Involvement

If relying on experts to draw (initial) district plans is a small
step from the status quo (particularly in the Iowa model),
independent redistricting commissions are more of a leap. In
chapter 4, I identified the various types of redistricting commissions that are currently in use in some parts of the United
States. Some of these commissions are merely advisory or are
used only as a backup, in the event that the legislature fails
to pass a redistricting plan. In those states that use advisory
or backup commissions, the legislature still has the power to
draw district lines. Since our concern is with alternatives to legislative redistricting, we will not consider advisory or backup
commissions in this chapter.

The focus here is on redistricting commissions that have

Table 6.1 States using Redistricting Commissions

State	Congressional	State legislative	Type	No. of members
Alaska	No	Yes	Political appointee	5
Arizona	Yes	Yes	Citizen	5
Arkansas	No	Yes	Politician	3
California	Yes	Yes	Citizen	14
Colorado	Yes	Yes	Citizen	12 / 12[a]
Hawaii	Yes	Yes	Political appointee	9
Idaho	Yes	Yes	Political appointee	6
Michigan	Yes	Yes	Citizen	13
Missouri	No	Yes	Political appointee[b]	20 (H) / 20 (S)
Montana	Yes[c]	Yes	Political appointee	5
New Jersey	Yes	Yes	Political appointee	13 / 10[d]
Ohio	No	Yes	Politician	7
Pennsylvania	No	Yes	Politician	5
Washington	Yes	Yes	Political appointee	5

[a] Colorado has separate commissions for congressional and state legislative redistricting.

[b] In Missouri, members of separate State House (H) and Senate (S) redistricting commissions are selected by the governor from lists submitted by the two main political parties.

[c] Montana has only one congressional district at the moment. If the state were awarded a second seat, as a result of reapportionment following the 2020 census, a redistricting commission would draw the district boundaries, as is currently done for state legislative districts.

[d] In New Jersey, there are 13 members of the redistricting committee responsible for congressional districts and 10 members of the committee that handles state legislative redistricting.

primary responsibility for drawing district boundaries (i.e., authority) and that are at least theoretically free of legislative influence (i.e., independence).[22] Currently, eight states use an independent redistricting commission (IRC) to draw both congressional and state legislative districts (though that number will rise to nine if Montana were to be awarded a second US House seat following 2020 reapportionment).[23] In another six states, including Montana currently, commissions are in charge of redrawing boundaries for state legislative districts only.[24] In total, then, there are 14 states in which independent commissions handle redistricting, all of which are listed in table 6.1.[25]

As noted in chapter 4, most of these commissions are what are known as "politician commissions." That is, their membership consists of "elected officials or their designees."[26] In table 6.1, I make a distinction between the two and label them "politician" and "political appointee" commissions, respectively. The three politician commissions are in Arkansas, Ohio, and Pennsylvania. The Arkansas Board of Apportionment is independent of the legislature in that it consists solely of three executive branch officials: the governor, secretary of state, and attorney general.

While a commission and not the entire legislature is responsible for state legislative redistricting in Ohio and Pennsylvania, legislators do serve on the commissions in these states. As a result, those commissions are not entirely independent of the legislature. The Ohio Redistricting Commission will be in charge of the legislative redistricting process for the first time in 2021. Membership on that commission combines three executive branch officials – the governor, auditor, and secretary of state – with four legislative appointees of the majority and minority leaders of the General Assembly. Interestingly, in order for the commission's redistricting plan to remain in effect for an entire decade, the two members of the committee from the minority legislative party must support the plan; if they do not, the plan is in effect for only four years.[27] The Pennsylvania Legislative Reapportionment Commission is perhaps the least independent of the 14 commissions listed in table 6.1 because four of the five members are legislators. They are, specifically, the leaders of the two parties in the State House and State Senate (with a fifth member selected by those four or appointed by the State Supreme Court if they cannot agree on the fifth member).

Seven commissions are populated with members who are appointed by politicians. Six of these seek a partisan balance among their members, though in four of those – Hawaii, Montana, New Jersey (for the congressional commission), and Washington – the even number of members selected for partisan balance themselves select an additional member. Only Alaska allows for partisan imbalance as the commission there consists of two selections by the governor and one each by the president of the Senate, the speaker of the House and the chief justice of the State Supreme Court. In none of the political appointee commissions can public officials serve as members.

The most independent of all redistricting commissions are the "independent citizen commissions" that currently exist in four states. These commissions have become the gold standard for reform among organizations advocating for changes to the redistricting process. As the Campaign Legal Center explains,

> Independent redistricting commissions appear to be the best and most workable solution to the plethora of problems created by incumbent legislative redistricting. When properly designed, independent commissions lend greater public legitimacy to the redistricting process and minimize the conflicts of interest that are otherwise inherent in redistricting.[28]

What distinguishes citizen commissions from the others in table 6.1 is the fact that their formation starts with a pool of potential members that elected officials do not create. Indeed, in all four states that utilize citizen commissions, interested citizens apply to be commissioners. Though each state uses a different method for selection of commission members, the critical element of these commissions is that their members "are not legislators and have no political ties that would compromise their judgment as commissioners; they are structurally incentivized to redistrict according to the values espoused by state law rather than self-interest."[29]

The first of these "independent citizen commissions" was established in Arizona when voters approved the new system by ballot initiative in 2000. There, the process begins when "a nonpartisan independent agency, the Commission on Appellate Court Appointments, screens applications from interested Arizonans and generates a list of qualified candidates – 10 Republicans, 10 Democrats, and five independents."[30] Next, two Republicans and two Democrats are selected from this list by legislative leaders from both parties. Finally, the four partisan commissioners choose an independent from the list to serve as the fifth commissioner.[31]

California voters adopted their own citizen redistricting commission for state legislative districts in 2008 (and gave the commission responsibility for congressional district boundaries in 2010). As in Arizona, registered voters who are interested in serving on the California Citizens Redistricting Commission may apply to do so.[32] Once applicants with conflicts of interest are removed, a three-person, multi-partisan Applicant Review Panel selects a maximum of 120 applicants, distributed equally in three "subpools" based on party affiliation. Those applicants are then interviewed by the review panel and 60 "of the most qualified . . . are presented to legislative leaders, who can strike up to 24 applicants."[33] At that point, the State Auditor randomly picks three Republican, three Democratic, and two other applicants from those remaining on the list. The final step occurs when the original eight commissioners themselves select two more applicants from each of the three party subpools, for a total of 14 commissioners.

The most recent states to adopt independent citizen redistricting commissions are Colorado and Michigan, each of which established their commissions following the success of ballot measures in 2018. In Colorado, there are separate commissions for congressional and state legislative redistricting. The Secretary of State and nonpartisan staffers review citizen applications for eligibility. Once those not eligible to serve have been eliminated from the pool, a three-person panel of retired Colorado Supreme Court justices and/or Colorado Court of Appeals judges, not all of the same party, randomly selects 300 applicants from each of the two largest parties in the state and 450 unaffiliated applicants. Next, the panel holds public hearings, "after which it will select 50 people from each initial pool who best demonstrate experience in representing the interests of groups or associations in Colorado, relevant analytical skills, ability to be impartial, and ability to promote consensus on the commission."[34] This is followed by the random drawing of two applicants from each of the three pools. Once these six commissioners are chosen, legislative leaders of both parties in both chambers each select ten applicants and pass their names to the judicial panel, which then selects one commissioner from each legislative leader's list. The panel then picks two unaffiliated commissioners from the original pool of 450 randomly-drawn applicants, bringing the total number of commissioners to twelve.[35] To approve a redistricting plan, eight of the twelve commissioners, including at least two who are unaffiliated, must support it.[36]

In Michigan, the Secretary of State solicits applications to serve on the Independent Citizens Redistricting Commission from the entire citizenry but also mails applications to 10,000 randomly selected Michigan residents. Once all applications have been submitted, 200 are selected randomly; 60 of these are Democrats, 60 are Republican, and 80 are unaffiliated. At that point, legislative leaders of both parties, in both chambers, may each strike five applicants from the 200 for any reason. Of the remaining applicants, the Secretary of State's Office will randomly select four Democratic, four Republican, and five unaffiliated commissioners, for a total of 13.[37] For a redistricting plan to be approved, a majority vote of the commission is required; at least two commissioners from each party and two unaffiliated commissioners must be in the majority.[38]

In all but one of these states, citizen commissions were established through ballot initiatives (Colorado's commissions were established via referenda). Essentially, an initiative allows citizens to bypass the state legislature by proposing statutes, and in some cases constitutional amendments, for voters' consideration. The constitutionality of commissions created by initiative was challenged in the 2015 Supreme Court case of *Arizona State Legislature v. Arizona Independent Redistricting Commission*.[39] The Arizona Legislature argued that the Elections Clause of the US Constitution – which states that "The Times, Places and Manner of holding Elections for Senators and Representatives shall be prescribed in each State by the Legislature thereof" – requires that state legislatures draw congressional district boundaries. In a 5-4 decision, the Supreme Court ruled against the Arizona Legislature, noting that "redistricting is a legislative function, to be performed in accordance with the State's prescriptions for lawmaking." In Arizona, those prescriptions include the initiative, so an independent citizens commission created by initiative may draw congressional district maps.

To reiterate, IRCs are given the authority to draw district boundaries but vary in the level of independence they have from the state legislature. Politician commissions are the least independent, followed by political appointee commissions, and then citizen commissions. Citizen commissions are currently the most prominent reform idea precisely because they have primary responsibility for redistricting while being almost entirely independent of influence from the legislature.

We might ask, however, whether IRCs are able to achieve the goals reformers set for them. Of course, there are a variety of goals for redistricting reform. If the goal is simply to avoid the apparent conflict of interest created by legislators drawing their own district boundaries, these commissions do so almost by definition. That's particularly true for citizen, and even political appointee, commissions. Transparency and widespread public participation are two more goals often held by reformers. Surely citizen and politician appointee commissions are more likely to accomplish those goals than legislatures, though that may depend on how the commissions are designed.[40]

Barry Edwards and colleagues have analyzed IRCs to determine whether they were better than state legislatures at "drawing compact districts, maintaining continuity, and respecting political subdivisions," each of which is often said to be a goal of redistricting reform.[41] They found evidence that both congressional and state legislative districts are more compact and split fewer counties and cities when drawn by IRCs than when they're drawn by legislatures.[42] When it comes to preserving as much of a previous district's population core as possible (i.e., continuity), IRCs do a better job than legislatures with respect to state legislative districts. However, there is no significant difference between the two in preserving the continuity of congressional districts.[43]

Perhaps the most common goal held by reformers is to increase the number of competitive districts. In chapter 5, we reviewed the research on the effect of redistricting commissions on electoral competition. Some of that work found that commissions either had no effect or reduced the level of competition when compared to redistricting by a unified legislature.[44] However, far more of the research finds that commissions enhance competition.[45] As Jamie Carson, Michael

Crespin, and Ryan Williamson concluded, "If states wish to increase competition in their congressional districts, utilizing commissions (or courts) when redistricting is an option that should be considered."[46]

It would appear, then, that IRCs help to accomplish most, if not all, of the goals of those seeking to reform the redistricting process. There are, however, those who have questioned the value of IRCs given the inability to hold them accountable for the maps they produce. Such critics point to the fact that there is no mechanism, such as an election, to punish commissioners for producing district maps that are unpopular with the voting public. As the argument goes, the alleged strength of the design of IRCs – namely, that the process is shielded from political influence – is actually their fatal flaw. As Michael Kang put it, "Insulation helps ensure that redistricting [by IRCs] is not driven by political self-interest, but it also ensures that redistricting is far removed from the necessary degree of public engagement, scrutiny, and accountability."[47]

The accountability argument is typically used to preserve the status quo of redistricting by legislatures (though, as we'll see, Kang proposes a direct democracy twist). Accountability, though, is hardly a virtue of the status quo. As Steven Huefner points out, "there is an obvious irony ... in wanting those who draw the maps to be accountable to the voters, while at the same time letting them draw their own maps even in self-interested ways that often deliberately reduce voters' abilities to defeat them on Election Day!"[48] For that reason, Huefner favors bringing the public into the redistricting process, as both political appointee and, especially, citizen redistricting commissions do. In this way, the public is given "a form of direct accountability, by putting voters, rather than perceived elites, in charge."[49] When a representative subset of the public draws the maps, it is as if the public itself is creating the districts in which they'll vote. The design of IRCs, therefore, must ensure that the selection process produces commissioners who are representative of the broader public. To the extent that they are, the demand for an accountable IRC is satisfied.

The availability of mapmaking software and personal computers that can process large amounts of data means that citizens can easily be involved in the process, even if they don't serve as commissioners. One way they've been encouraged to do so is by entering redistricting competitions sponsored by reform organizations. As noted in chapter 4, these competitions rely on publicly available programs, such as DistrictBuilder, that allow citizens to draw their own district boundaries based on commonly applied redistricting values such as district compactness, electoral competition, or minority representation.[50] Ideally, winning citizen-drawn maps could be compared to maps drawn by legislatures to call attention to gerrymanders.

Reform groups in Ohio held innovative redistricting competitions in 2009 and 2011 in which the public was invited to submit maps that were scored according to a formula devised by the sponsors and based on several district criteria that reformers believe are important. These include compactness, county integrity, partisan fairness, and competitiveness. Altman and McDonald analyzed the congressional district maps that were submitted in the 2011 competition and compared them to three plans drawn by legislators, including the plan that was ultimately adopted. In addition to the criteria in the competition formula, Altman and McDonald also compared plans in terms of minority representation and population equality.[51] They found that, on average, plans submitted by the public "score better than the adopted [legislative] plan on compactness, county integrity, partisan balance, and district competitiveness" and had a better overall score.[52] Importantly, the public plans scored high on all criteria while also ensuring minority representation (in one largely African American district), which means that "reformers' goals can be achieved harmoniously with the voting rights community's goals."[53] In the end, the Ohio experiment suggests that citizens are more than capable of drawing district maps that meet criteria many people believe vital to a fair electoral system.

It's worth noting that the public could have a role in redistricting even if legislatures remained in control of the process. Recognizing the need for redistricting reform, Kang suggests that plans drawn by a legislature should be required to win approval of the electorate at large through a direct vote. Specifically, he proposes that legislators vote on alternative redistricting plans and that the two receiving the most votes be placed, head-to-head, in front of the voters for their decision.[54] This use of direct democracy in the redistricting process would, ideally, "induce the major parties to forsake the maximization of political advantage and to compete instead for the median voter's approval."[55] It also represents something of a compromise "between skeptics who would leave redistricting completely to the legislature despite the costs, and reformers who would sequester redistricting completely from the political process."[56]

Whether through IRCs, public mapping competitions, or direct votes on legislative maps, state legislatures' monopoly over redistricting is increasingly being challenged. Indeed, the public appears supportive of any effort to wrest control of redistricting from legislators. In 2018, there were six reform measures on the ballot in five states, including the citizen commissions in Colorado and Michigan. All six measures passed and, with the exception of the advisory commission in Utah (which passed with 50.34 percent of the vote), did so with the support of overwhelming majorities.

Multimember Districts

The most radical break with how redistricting is currently done in the United States would be to move from single-member to multimember legislative districts. It should be noted this would be "radical" only in the American context. The majority of democracies in the world utilize multimember districts for at least a portion of their legislatures.

Depending on how large the multimember districts would be, and on how they were configured, this reform could eliminate redistricting altogether. Obviously, multimember districts would allow for fewer districts overall. Fewer districts, in turn, require fewer lines to be drawn. For example, if a state with ten single-member districts created two districts with five representatives in each, only a single line dividing the two districts would be necessary. Multimember districts could consist of two or three representatives each or might consist of dozens or even hundreds of representatives (chosen, for example, statewide or in one large national district).

The vast majority of legislative districts in the United States are single-member districts. That means, quite simply, that there is one, and only one, representative per district. Though single-member congressional districts were theoretically mandated as early as 1842, for a variety of reasons multimember districts existed in some states until the middle of the twentieth century. It was not until 1967 that federal law finally required single-member congressional districts.[57] Thus, if the public, and its lawmakers, wished to once again allow multimember districts, they would not need to amend the Constitution and could do so by merely changing the law.

State law determines whether state legislative districts can contain multiple representatives. Currently, only ten states utilize multimember districts, though one of these – West Virginia

– recently passed legislation to switch to single-member districts following the 2020 Census.[58] Most states using multi-member districts allow no more than two representatives per district. Some districts in Maryland's House of Delegates have three representatives (while others have just one or two); Vermont has state Senate districts with as many as six senators; and there are 400 members of the New Hampshire House of Representatives in 204 districts, with the number per district ranging from one to 11.[59]

Part of the impetus for shifting to single-member districts beginning in the mid-twentieth century was the concern that multimember districts made it difficult for racial minorities to elect their candidates of choice. At-large elections – where all representatives in a city or county are elected citywide or countywide – were often used to dilute minority voting strength. If, for instance, five city council members were to be elected citywide, and voters were given five votes each, five candidates from the majority group were very likely to win all the seats (assuming the majority group voted as a bloc, which white voters typically did when minority candidates were on the ballot). There is considerable evidence that multimember districts make it harder to achieve minority representation, at least in certain circumstances.[60] However, some recent scholarship calls this conclusion into question.[61] As Paul Herrnson and his co-authors suggest, older studies on this topic may have failed to disentangle the consequences of multimember districts from oppressive tactics used in the past "such as racial gerrymandering and voter intimidation."[62] It's possible, too, that as the power of partisanship increasingly influences voting decisions, the race of candidates is playing less of a role than it did several decades ago. Regardless, there are systems of voting that could be implemented to help protect the interests of voters who find themselves in a numerical minority of any sort.

As the previous chapter indicated, the consequences of gerrymandering are not entirely clear. There is certainly evidence that gerrymandering is to blame for the lack of competition in American elections, for the partisan bias we often see in election outcomes, and for the growth in polarization in recent years. But there is also evidence that gerrymandering does not contribute (at least not much) to these problems. What is clear is that single-member districts, particularly when coupled with plurality voting (i.e., a system in which the candidate with the most votes wins), often produces a disproportionate number of seats won in a legislature when compared to the number of votes a party receives.[63] Such districts also produce a potentially large number of voters who support a losing candidate and are, therefore, represented in the legislature (or at least one chamber in the legislature) by someone who does not share their partisan perspective. This is particularly problematic for those who believe that democratic representation requires representative institutions to reflect the policy preferences of the public. Because political parties act (in part) as proxies for policy preferences in modern, mass democracies, the partisan makeup of a legislature ought to mirror the level of support for various parties (including, perhaps, minor parties) within the public. This view is at the root of concerns about partisan biases in elections.

Of course, many others believe that representation requires elected officials to protect the interests of people living in particular areas. Cities may differ from rural areas in their demands; agricultural areas might have different interests than industrial areas; and wealthy areas will have different concerns than working-class areas, to name but a few possible distinctions between localities. Given these differences, and their importance to the lives of people living in various places, some would argue that territorial (or "corporate") representation must be preserved. Recall from chapter 2, and our discussion of the work of Rosemarie Zagarri, that this perspective dates to the American colonial period, when "the colonists drew on their English experience in devising methods of representation."[64] The assumption was, and is, "that physical proximity generate[s] communal sentiment," which is why, "In England, counties, boroughs, and universities had been the basis of representation."[65]

Perhaps we would all prefer to have both fair partisan representation as well as effective territorial representation. While this may be possible (using a method I'll discuss later in this section), there is a deep tension between the two types of representation. As James Gardner argues, "party and territory are conflicting and for the most part incommensurable principles upon which to found a system of legislative representation."[66] This is simply because a single representative, from a particular area of a state or country, cannot accurately reflect the partisan preferences of all his or her constituents. Indeed, 100 percent of the representation in a single-member district (i.e., one seat) goes to a party with support from often far less than 100 percent of the voters. Of course, disproportionality exists in every single-member district and some of it will balance out when representation is aggregated across an entire state or country. Still, a system of single-member representation, designed in large part to represent places, will not be particularly good at reflecting the partisan preferences of the electorate just as a system designed to represent partisan preferences is not able to represent specific places very well.

In other words, a system of representation must typically prioritize one view of representation over the other. Those who prefer the attention to local concerns that territorial representation provides are not likely to favor multimember districts as these districts are usually larger than single-member districts. This is not necessarily the case, it should be said, though the creation of geographically small multimember districts would likely require a legislature with more representatives than would come from comparably sized single-member districts. To illustrate, imagine a legislature with 100 small, single-member districts. Such a legislature, obviously, consists of 100 representatives. To convert those 100 districts to similarly small multimember districts of, say, three representatives each would require a legislature of 300 representatives. Thus, multimember districts are likely to cover larger geographical areas so as not to necessitate legislatures with an unwieldy number of representatives. To the extent that multimember districts are larger, and therefore broaden the territory to be represented, those preferring territorial representation are unlikely to be satisfied with them.

The opposite may be true for those who prefer that legislatures be representative of the partisan preferences of the public. Of course, that really depends on whether multimember districts do, in fact, produce legislatures in which the number of seats a party controls is proportional to its share of support in the electorate. So do multimember districts produce more proportional results than single-member districts? At this point, we must introduce a complicating factor, namely, the state's (or country's) electoral system, or "the set of rules that structure how votes are cast at elections for a representative assembly and how these votes are then converted into seats in that assembly."[67] Electoral systems are the subject of a tremendous amount of research and the present book has neither the scope nor the space to explore that research in any detail. What follows, then, is a simplified discussion of "two of the most important voting methods from a theoretical standpoint and in terms of the frequency of their use in the world's major democracies."[68]

Those two voting methods, or electoral systems, are plurality and proportional elections.[69] In the former, the candidate (or candidates) with the most votes wins the election. A plurality is not necessarily a majority (50 percent plus one) of the vote; it is simply more votes than any other candidate. So, for example, in a race with three candidates, the winning candidate could theoretically have as little as 34 percent of the vote. Plurality elections most often are used in systems with single-member districts but it is possible to use plurality voting in multimember districts. If three seats are to be filled in a district, plurality voting would mean that the three candidates with the most votes would win. (Voters may be given a single vote in such elections or they can be given more than one.)

In systems using proportional election methods (i.e. proportional representation or "PR"), the winning parties are allocated seats according to (roughly) the percentage of the vote they received in the election. Thus, in a district with 10 representatives, a party winning 40 percent of the vote would get four seats and two parties winning 30 percent of the vote would each get three seats. The essential element of any proportional system is that it must use multimember districts since, obviously, a single seat can't be split proportionally. It is also important to note that PR is very likely to foster a system with more than two political parties while single-member plurality has a tendency to produce two-party systems.[70]

Why is this brief discussion of plurality and proportional electoral systems relevant? Because the effect of the number of seats per district (or what political scientists call "district magnitude") may depend on the electoral system in use. There is no doubt that PR produces more proportional results than the single-member plurality system. Such a comparison suggests that a larger district magnitude (which PR has, by definition, compared to single-member plurality) leads to more proportional outcomes. But what if we were to use a multimember plurality system? There is some evidence that as district magnitude increases in plurality systems, proportionality actually decreases.[71] However, Andrew Eggers and Alexander Fouirnaies find that the connection between district magnitude and proportionality of election results in plurality systems is somewhat complicated and depends on whether one examines district magnitude at the district or systemwide level. The main conclusion of their analysis is that increasing the number of representatives per district marginally increases proportionality in plurality systems, while increasing the number of representatives per district and holding the total number of representatives fixed (systemwide) is likely to decrease proportionality.[72]

Keep in mind that the goal for redistricting reformers is to reduce the opportunities for gerrymandering. Assuming they also would prefer to see legislatures more closely reflect partisan divisions in the electorate – or would like to see the emergence of "third parties" with representation in the legislature – they ought to advocate for multimember districts using PR. There is no other way to simultaneously reduce the number of districts that have to be drawn and achieve proportionality in election outcomes. (If multimember districts were to be coupled with plurality voting, Eggers and Fouirnaies suggest that increased proportionality is possible only by keeping the number of districts relatively constant while increasing the total number of legislators. But keeping the number of districts constant undermines the goal of reducing the amount of redistricting to be conducted.)

How might a state, or the entire country, implement multimember districts using PR? A relatively small state might opt to elect all of its representatives statewide; larger states might split the state in half or in thirds. If, for example, Pennsylvania wanted to maintain its current number of 203 state representatives, who are currently elected in 203 single-member districts, it could decide to divide the state essentially in the middle, with one half of the state electing 102 representatives and the other (slightly smaller) half electing 101. Or it could divide the state into three districts with 68 representatives from two of the districts and 67 from the third.

For Congress, states would have similar choices. For example, Pennsylvania, which currently has 18 members of the House of Representatives (though is likely to lose one seat after the 2020 reapportionment), could use PR to elect all 18 statewide; it could divide the state in half and elect nine per district; or it could divide the state in thirds and elect six per district. Of course, multimember districts would not be possible in states with only one representative and it would be relatively ineffective in states with only two or three representatives. This reform would require only a change in federal law, and corresponding changes to state law, to allow for multimember congressional districts.

A more radical proposal – requiring a Constitutional amendment – would be to elect members of the House regionally. That is, the country could be divided into four, five or more regions, with equal numbers of representatives elected, using PR, per regional "district." District lines could follow state boundaries to avoid the need to redistrict but this would require a relaxing of the requirement that districts have perfectly equal population sizes. Alternatively, district lines could be drawn to ensure equal population but this would mean that regional district lines would have to be drawn and they would inevitably split parts of some states into different regions. More radical still would be to elect all 435 members of the House nationwide.

For a variety of reasons, electoral reform is difficult to accomplish.[73] In the context of the United States, a shift to PR would be particularly difficult given widespread animosity toward

political parties and the long history, discussed earlier, of territorial representation. Many Americans would simply not want
to sacrifice local representation for more proportional partisan
representation. Fortunately, a compromise option is available. Mixed-member electoral systems are a popular reform
idea and are used in several countries, including Germany and
New Zealand.[74] Without getting into too much detail, mixed-
member systems elect part of the legislature in single-member
districts, typically according to plurality rules (although majority rules can apply), and the other part in multimember
districts using PR. Voters cast two votes – one for a candidate
in their single-member district and another for a party in the
multimember district. The system can be designed in such a
way that the results of the PR election are independent of the
single-member district results or they can be linked so that the
PR results compensate for disproportionality in the single-
member elections. The advantage of the latter approach, called
a mixed-member proportional (or "MMP") system, is that it
can accomplish the goals of both those who want to preserve
territorial representation and those who want fair partisan
representation. A disadvantage, which is particularly relevant
to this book, is that district lines still have to be drawn around
all the single-member districts. As a result, an MMP system
might not reduce gerrymandering at all, though it would correct in the aggregate for partisan bias that might be produced
by gerrymandering the single-member districts.

There are, of course, complications with all of the
aforementioned reforms and no system is capable of producing
only positive results. There are trade-offs whenever political
reform is undertaken.[75] Nevertheless, multimember districts,
particularly when coupled with PR, reduce the opportunities
for gerrymandering (if not eliminating them altogether) and
ensure proportional representation for political parties. To the

extent that those are the ultimate goals of redistricting reformers, PR is the ideal approach.

Conclusion

This chapter has reviewed several potential reforms that would alter, or perhaps eliminate altogether, redistricting in the United States. They include the use of non-partisan bureaucrats to draw district lines that are then submitted to either the legislature or a redistricting committee for approval; the use of redistricting committees, with varying levels of independence from legislators and elected officials generally, to establish district boundaries; and the use of multimember districts with proportional electoral rules. None of these should be viewed as a silver bullet, capable of transforming the American electoral system into a perfectly functioning democracy. There are serious problems with elections in the United States, and with the political system more broadly, that have nothing to do with gerrymandering (e.g., campaign finance).

Still, gerrymandering is viewed by most Americans as a blight on the system. Regardless of the measurable consequences of gerrymandering, reform of the system is a critical step in beginning to rebuild faith in elections. Recent successful attempts to create citizens redistricting commissions suggests that significant portions of the public are eager to upend the status quo.

This book is intended as a general introduction to redistricting and gerrymandering in the United States. We've considered theoretical, historical, and legal aspects of the process and described its operation. We've also examined the empirical research on the subject, from which we've learned that the findings are often conflicting and clear conclusions are elusive. Finally, we've offered reform alternatives. Whether the aim is to defend the current system of redistricting or to change it, a rich understanding of how that system works will be needed. Part of that understanding must be a recognition that redistricting is a political process and, thus, debates over its preservation or transformation are also political. To say the process is political is to say that, regardless of the outcome of those debates, there will be winners and there will be losers. This fact should not discourage those who would seek to improve our system of representative democracy but should brace them for the long, difficult work required to achieve political change of any sort.

Further Reading

This book serves as a general overview of gerrymandering and the redistricting process. As such, it builds on previous introductory work that is now somewhat dated. Nevertheless, much of this earlier work is still worth consulting. In particular, David Butler and Bruce Cain's *Congressional Redistricting: Comparative and Theoretical Perspectives* (1991) remains a valuable treatment of the conceptual elements of redistricting. More recently, Charles Bullock's *Redistricting: The Most Political Activity in America* (2010) is a comprehensive review of the process as it existed prior to the 2010 round of redistricting.

The 2010 redistricting cycle produced what many observers believe to be particularly egregious examples of gerrymandering. Journalist David Daley's *Ratf**ked: The True Story Behind the Secret Plan to Steal America's Democracy* (2017) provides a descriptive account of Republican efforts to draw districts for partisan advantage. Those efforts are explored in a documentary film, *Slay the Dragon* (Durrance and Goodman 2020), which also highlights the reform movement that emerged in response.

Those interested in the history of gerrymandering have precious few sources to consult. Elmer Griffith's doctoral dissertation, *The Rise and Development of the Gerrymander* (1907), is useful for information on early experiments with gerrymandering. Otherwise, Rosemarie Zagarri's *The*

Politics of Size (1987) and Peverill Squire's *The Evolution of American Legislatures* (2012) provide insight into how legislative districts have been envisioned historically, and Michel Balinski and H. Peyton Young's *Fair Representation* (2001) explores changing approaches to apportionment over time. Of course, Erik Engstrom's empirical analysis of gerrymandering, *Partisan Gerrymandering and the Construction of American Democracy* (2016) extends to the early republic and contains rich historical data.

The impact of redistricting on the quality of representation commands quite a bit of attention in the academic literature. Though the assumption among many is that gerrymandering hinders representation by undermining competitive elections, some – like Thomas Brunell in *Redistricting and Representation* (2008) and Justin Buchler in "Competition, Representation, and Redistricting" (2005) – argue that representation is enhanced when districts are drawn to be safe for one party. Similarly, in "The Paradox of Redistricting" (2011), Antoine Yoshinaka and Chad Murphy find that redistricting causes instability, which may foster competition but undermine the link between representatives and their constituents. Finally, Andrew Gelman and Gary King's "Enhancing Democracy Through Legislative Redistricting" (1994) demonstrates that the redistricting process increases the responsiveness of legislators not by creating safe seats but "by shaking up the political system and creating high levels of uncertainty for all participants" (543).

Though much of the recent anxiety about gerrymandering has focused on partisan bias, an earlier, and not altogether resolved, problem concerned race. The first attempt to rectify racial inequities in representation was the "reapportionment revolution" in the 1960s. J. Douglas Smith's *On Democracy's Doorstep* (2014) tells the story of the Supreme Court's path to the concept of "one person, one vote." In *The End of Inequality* (2008), Stephen Ansolabehere and James Snyder examine the system in place before the reapportionment cases of the 1960s and explain the constitutional underpinnings, as well as the political consequences, of the new system. A systematic analysis of those consequences is Gary Cox and Jonathan Katz's classic study *Elbridge Gerry's Salamander* (2002).

In the 1990s, majority-minority districts began to be widely used in an attempt to bolster representation for racial minorities or, at least, to avoid violating minority voting rights. This development led to a considerable amount of scholarly examination. Two important early studies in this area are David Lublin's *The Paradox of Representation* (1997) and David Canon's *Race, Redistricting, and Representation* (1999).

Of course, the bulk of the research conducted in this area attempts to determine the effects that redistricting, if not gerrymandering, has on elections. Some of the work notes that, while redistricting can be consequential, those drawing maps often face constraints that limit their ability to produce heavily biased districts. Jonathan Winburn's *The Realities of Redistricting* (2008) makes such a point with respect to state legislative districts, while Nicholas Seabrook's *Drawing the Lines* (2017) does so for congressional districts.

Early work on the electoral effects of redistricting was often skeptical that effects were large. Mark Rush's *Does Redistricting Make a Difference?* (1993) is a key example. More recently, Engstrom's *Partisan Gerrymandering and the Construction of American Democracy* (2016) and *Gerrymandering in America* (2016) by Anthony McGann, Charles Anthony Smith, Michael Latner, and Alex Keena provide rigorous empirical analyses of gerrymandering and find that the practice does produce significant effects. Interestingly, McGann and colleagues maintain that it's only after the Supreme Court's decision in *Vieth v.*

Jubelirer (2004) that such effects emerge. That decision, they write, made it possible "to take partisan gerrymandering to its limits" (p. 16). Indeed, parties are likely to do so in those states where there is political motive (i.e., elections are highly competitive) and the opportunity to do so exists (i.e., one party has unified control of state government).

Political scientists are not the only scholars who have shown an interest in redistricting and gerrymandering. In addition to some mathematicians (see Duchin 2018 for a popular explanation of the role of mathematicians in redistricting court cases), geographers have occasionally taken up the subject. *Seats, Votes, and the Spatial Organization of Elections* (1979) by Graham Gudgin and Peter Taylor is a classic study of the impact of geography, including district boundaries, on the relationship between seats and votes. Far more accessible, and more recent, is Mark Monmonier's *Bushmanders & Bullwinkles* (2001). Monmonier's book is a study in cartography, or "an examination of how legislators, redistricting officials, and constitutional lawyers use maps as both tools and weapons" (x).

Those seeking alternatives to the current system of redistricting might look to other countries for models. To that end, Bernard Grofman and Lisa Handley's edited volume *Redistricting in Comparative Perspective* (2008) should be consulted. On redistricting commissions, Bruce Cain's 2012 article "Redistricting Commissions: A Better Political Buffer" is a good place to start (though see also Edwards et al., "Can Independent Redistricting Commissions Lead Us out of the Political Thicket," 2016). Finally, in *The Public Mapping Project* (2018), Michael McDonald and Micah Altman outline the way in which the public can participate directly in the redistricting process through easy-to-use and publicly available redistricting software.

Notes

CHAPTER 1. WHAT'S THE PROBLEM?

1 Wang, Sam. 2013. "The Great Gerrymander of 2012." *The New York Times*, February 2. https://www.nytimes.com/2013/02/03/opinion/sunday/the-great-gerrymander-of-2012.html (accessed July 17, 2019).

2 Emamdjomeh, Armand, Ann Gerhart, and Tim Meko. 2018. "Why North Carolina's House district lines have been upended – again." *The Washington Post*, August 31. https://www.washingtonpost.com/graphics/2018/politics/north-carolina-redistricting/ (accessed August 21, 2019).

3 Campaign Legal Center press release, January 25, 2019. https://campaignlegal.org/sites/default/files/2019-01/CLC%20Bipartisan%20Redistrictig%20Poll.pdf

4 Ibid.

5 Grofman, Bernard and Lisa Handley. 2008. "Introduction: Redistricting in Comparative Perspective." In *Redistricting in Comparative Perspective*, eds. Bernard Grofman and Lisa Handley (New York: Oxford University Press), 3–8.

6 Burnett, Kristin D. 2001. "Congressional Apportionment: 2010 Census Briefs," United States Department of Commerce, US Census Bureau, 4. https://www.census.gov/content/dam/Census/library/publications/2011/dec/c2010br-08.pdf (accessed July 18, 2019).

7 The exceptions are states with only one representative, since state boundaries serve as the congressional district lines.

8 For a comprehensive list, see Appendix A in Grofman and Handley.

9 Johnston, Ron, Charles Pattie, and David Rossiter. 2008. "Electoral Distortion Despite Redistricting by Independent Commissions: The British Case, 1950–2005." In *Redistricting in Comparative*

Perspective, eds. Bernard Grofman and Lisa Handley (New York: Oxford University Press), 218.

10 Ibid., 219.

11 For a classic treatment of this phenomenon, see Rae, Douglas W. 1967. *The Political Consequences of Electoral Laws*. New Haven, CT: Yale University Press.

12 Johnston et al., "Electoral Distortion Despite Redistricting by Independent Commissions," 205.

13 Though it is possible to unintentionally produce biased maps, we are concerned with deliberate efforts to manipulate the process for partisan ends.

14 On this point, generally, see Crick, Bernard. 2005. *In Defense of Politics*. New York: Continuum.

15 Some may also break the law in pursuit of their ends but we should not expect, and certainly should not accept, such behavior.

16 Grofman and Handley, "Introduction," 3.

17 Elklit, Jørgen and Palle Svensson. 1997. "What Makes Elections Free and Fair?" *The Journal of Democracy* 8: 35. See also Dahl, Robert A. 1989. *Democracy and Its Critics*. New Haven, CT: Yale University Press, 221.

18 Elklit and Svensson, "What Makes Elections Free and Fair?," 35.

19 Ibid.

20 Thompson, Dennis F. 2002. *Just Elections: Creating a Fair Electoral Process in the United States*. Chicago, IL: The University of Chicago Press, 2.

21 Ibid.

22 Buchler, Justin. 2010. "The Inevitability of Gerrymandering: Winners and Losers Under Alternative Approaches to Redistricting." *Duke Journal of Constitutional Law & Public Policy* 5: 18–19 (emphasis mine).

23 Ibid., 19.

24 Ibid., 20.

25 Ibid., 30–3.

26 Williamson, Kevin D. 2017. "In Praise of Gerrymandering." *National Review*, June 21. https://www.nationalreview.com/2017/06/gerrymandering-supreme-court-case-redistricting-legislature-republicans-democrats/

27 Ibid. For a scholarly argument against judicial interference in incumbent-protection gerrymandering, see Persily, Nathaniel.

2002. "In Defense of Foxes Guarding Henhouses: The Case for Judicial Acquiescence to Incumbent-Protecting Gerrymanders." *Harvard Law Review* 116: 649–83.

28 The distinction between "normal politics" and "constitutional politics" was first drawn by Bruce Ackerman though not in the context of redistricting. The distinction is part of his theory of "dualist democracy." See Ackerman, Bruce. 1991. *We The People: Foundations.* Cambridge, MA: The Belknap Press.

29 Lasswell, Harold D. 1936. *Politics: Who Gets What, When, How.* New York: McGraw-Hill.

30 Alexander, Larry and Saikrishna B. Prakash. 2008. "Tempest in an Empty Teapot: Why the Constitution Does Not Regulate Gerrymandering." *William and Mary Law Review* 50: 46–7.

31 There is a large philosophical literature on public reason and reasonableness. The classic statement, however, is found in Rawls, John. 1993. *Political Liberalism.* New York: Columbia University Press, 48–54.

32 Quong, Jonathan. 2004. "The Scope of Public Reason." *Political Studies* 52: 248–9, n. 1.

33 Issacharoff, Samuel and Richard Pildes. 1998. "Politics as Markets: Partisan Lockups of the Democratic Process." *Stanford Law Review* 50: 643. See also Pildes, Richard H. 1999. "The Theory of Political Competition." *Virginia Law Review* 85: 1605–26; and Issacharoff, Samuel. 2000. "Oversight of Regulated Political Markets." *Harvard Journal of Law & Public Policy* 24: 91–102.

34 Issacharoff and Pildes, "Politics as Markets," 648.

35 Ibid., 646.

36 Issacharoff, Samuel. 2002. "Gerrymandering and Political Cartels." *Harvard Law Review* 116: 600.

37 Ibid., 599.

38 See Levitt, Justin and Michael P. McDonald. 2007. "Taking the 'Re' Out of Redistricting: State Constitutional Provisions on Redistricting Timing." *Georgetown Law Journal* 95: 1247–86.

39 See, for example, Huefner, Steven F. 2010. "Don't Just Make Redistricters *More Accountable* to the People, Make *Them* the People." *Duke Journal of Constitutional Law & Public Policy* 5: 37–67; and Kang, Michael S. 2006. "De-Rigging Elections: Direct Democracy and the Future of Redistricting Reform." *Washington University Law Review* 84: 667–716.

40 That is, unless it is part of a type of politics Mark Tushnet calls "constitutional hardball," which occurs, according to Tushnet, during times of constitutional transformation. See Tushnet, Mark V. 2004. "Constitutional Hardball." *The John Marshall Law Review* 37: 523–53. That might be a difficult case to make, given the long history of gerrymandering in the United States. However, one could argue that the particularly aggressive attempts to gerrymander districts following the 2010 census, especially by the Republican Party, amount to constitutional hardball. For an account of those efforts, see Daley, David. 2016. *Rat F**ked: Why Your Vote Doesn't Count*. New York: Liveright Publishing.

41 See the entry for "beanbag" in Safire, William. 2008. *Safire's Political Dictionary*, Updated and Expanded Edition. New York: Oxford University Press, 45–6.

42 For a very useful review, see Urbinati, Nadia and Mark E. Warren. 2008. "The Concept of Representation in Contemporary Democratic Theory." *Annual Review of Political Science* 11: 387–412. See also Mansbridge, Jane. 2003. "Rethinking Representation." *American Political Science Review* 97: 515–28.

43 Prior to the "reapportionment revolution" of the 1960s, most of the debate over redistricting would have concerned descriptive representation, particularly with respect to race.

44 Weissberg, Robert. 1978. "Collective vs. Dyadic Representation in Congress." *American Political Science Review* 72: 535. See also Hill, Kim Quaile and Patricia A. Hurley. 1999. "Dyadic Representation Reappraised." *American Journal of Political Science* 43: 109–37.

45 Buchler, Justin. 2005. "Competition, Representation and Redistricting: The Case Against Competitive Congressional Districts." *Journal of Theoretical Politics* 17: 431–63; Brunell, Thomas L. 2008. *Redistricting and Representation: Why Competitive Elections are Bad for America*. New York: Routledge; Buchler, Justin. 2011. *Hiring and Firing Public Officials: Rethinking the Purpose of Elections*. New York: Oxford University Press.

46 On the benefits of competitive elections, generally, see Lipsitz, Keena. 2011. *Competitive Elections and the American Voter*. Philadelphia, PA: University of Pennsylvania Press.

47 Weissberg, "Collective vs. Dyadic Representation in Congress," 536.

48 For a discussion of how collective representation is measured, see

Hurley, Patricia A. 1982. "Collective Representation Reappraised." *Legislative Studies Quarterly* 7: 119–36.

49 There is a very long literature on this phenomenon. For those interested, a good place to start would be Tufte, Edward R. 1973. "The Relationship between Seats and Votes in Two-Party Systems." *American Political Science Review* 67: 540–54; and Taagepera, Rein. 1973. "Seats and Votes: A Generalization of the Cube Law of Elections." *Social Science Research* 2: 257–75.

50 Ideally, from this perspective, seat distribution in the House of Representatives would match the aggregate national vote for House candidates. Of course, there is no controlling authority who could ensure that result, as redistricting is done on a state-by-state basis.

CHAPTER 2. A BRIEF HISTORY OF GERRYMANDERING

1 Squire, Peverill. 2012. *The Evolution of American Legislatures: Colonies, Territories, and States, 1619–2009*. Ann Arbor, MI: University of Michigan Press, 12; 15.

2 Ibid., 16–26.

3 Zagarri, Rosemarie. 1987. *The Politics of Size: Representation in the United States, 1776–1850*. Ithaca, NY: Cornell University Press, 37–8.

4 Quoted in Klain, Maurice. 1955. "A New Look at the Constituencies: The Need for a Recount and a Reappraisal." *American Political Science Review* 49: 1112.

5 Squire, *The Evolution of American Legislatures*, 15–16.

6 McKinley, Albert Edward. 1905. *The Suffrage Franchise in the Thirteen English Colonies in America*. Philadelphia, PA: Ginn and Company, 169.

7 Griffith, Elmer C. 1907. *The Rise and Development of the Gerrymander*. Chicago, IL: Scott, Foresman and Company, 23. In what follows, I will rely heavily on Griffith as it remains the most complete history of early American gerrymandering available.

8 Ibid., 25.

9 Ibid., 26.

10 Ibid., 26–8.

11 Lincoln, C. H. 1899. "Representation in the Pennsylvania Assembly

Prior to the Revolution." *The Pennsylvania Magazine of History and Biography* 23: 27.

12 Ibid., 27.
13 Griffith, *The Rise and Development of the Gerrymander*, 29.
14 Ibid., 28.
15 Ibid.
16 Squire, *The Evolution of American Legislatures*, 72–83.
17 Squire, Peverill. 2006. "Historical Evolution of Legislatures in the United States." *Annual Review of Political Science* 9: 21.
18 Ibid., 28.
19 Zagarri, *The Politics of Size*, 39.
20 Ibid., 36–7.
21 Ibid., 39.
22 Squire, "Historical Evolution of Legislatures in the United States," 28.
23 Griffith, *The Rise and Development of the Gerrymander*, 30.
24 Ibid.
25 Constitution of New York, 1777. Article XII. https://www.nycourts.gov/history/legal-history-new-york/documents/Publications_1777-NY-Constitution.pdf (accessed September 21, 2019).
26 Griffith, *The Rise and Development of the Gerrymander*, 31.
27 Klain, "A New Look at the Constituencies," 1111.
28 Zagarri, *The Politics of Size*, 107.
29 Ibid., 115.
30 Ibid., 116.
31 Ibid., 115–18.
32 Ibid., 107–12, and 118–20.
33 William Pitt Beers, as quoted in ibid., 120.
34 Ibid, 120–1.
35 Ibid., 121.
36 Griffith, *The Rise and Development of the Gerrymander*, 35–41. A more recent analysis, by Thomas Rogers Hunter, comes to a similar conclusion. Hunter, Thomas Rogers. 2011. "The First Gerrymander? Patrick Henry, James Madison, James Monroe, and Virginia's 1788 Congressional Districting." *Early American Studies* 9: 781–820.
37 Griffith, *The Rise and Development of the Gerrymander*, 43.
38 Ibid., 45.
39 Ibid., 45; 51–5.

40 Ibid., 46.
41 Ibid., 61.
42 Ibid., 64.
43 Ibid., 64–6.
44 Ibid., 63.
45 Ibid., 66.
46 Ibid., 72–3.
47 Ibid., 73.
48 Austin, James T. 1829. *The Life of Elbridge Gerry*, Volume 2. Boston, MA: Wells and Lilly, 347–8.
49 Ibid., 348.
50 Ibid.
51 Griffith, *The Rise and Development of the Gerrymander*, 73–4.
52 Engstrom, Erik J. 2013. *Partisan Gerrymandering and the Construction of American Democracy*. Ann Arbor, MI: University of Michigan Press, 31. What follows relies heavily on Engstrom as his is the only systematic analysis of gerrymandering in eras prior to the mid- to late twentieth century.
53 Ibid., 31; 32.
54 Ibid., 29.
55 Ibid., 32.
56 Ibid., 35–6.
57 Ibid., 38.
58 Ibid., 23.
59 See McCormick, Richard P. 1966. *The Second American Party System: Party Formation in the Jacksonian Era*. Chapel Hill, NC: University of North Carolina Press; and Silbey, Joel A. 1991. *The American Political Nation, 1838–1893*. Stanford, CA: Stanford University Press.
60 Engstrom, *Partisan Gerrymandering and the Construction of American Democracy*, 43.
61 Ibid., 44.
62 See, for example, Ross, Robert E. 2017. "Recreating the House: The 1842 Apportionment Act and the Whig Party's Reconstruction of Representation." *Polity* 49: 408–33. Zagarri discusses the Act in terms of the interests of small and large states; see Zagarri, *The Politics of Size*, 129–31.
63 Engstrom, *Partisan Gerrymandering and the Construction of American Democracy*, 62.

64 Ibid., 64–5.
65 Ross, Robert E. and Barrett Anderson. 2018. "Single-Member Districts Are Not Constitutionally Required." *Constitutional Commentary* 33: 285–6.
66 Engstrom, *Partisan Gerrymandering and the Construction of American Democracy*, 67–9.
67 Ibid., 72–5.
68 Ibid., 76.
69 Ibid., 90. See also Engstrom, Erik J. 2006. "Stacking the States, Stacking the House: The Partisan Consequences of Congressional Redistricting in the 19th Century." *American Political Science Review* 100: 419–27.
70 Engstrom, *Partisan Gerrymandering and the Construction of American Democracy*, 93.
71 Ibid., 103.
72 Ibid., 106–10.
73 Niemi, Richard G. and Patrick Fett. 1986. "The Swing Ratio: An Explanation and an Assessment." *Legislative Studies Quarterly* 11: 75–90.
74 Engstrom, *Partisan Gerrymandering and the Construction of American Democracy*, 110–14.
75 Ibid., 135–8.
76 Carson, Jamie L., Erik J. Engstrom, and Jason M. Roberts. 2006. "Redistricting, Candidate Entry, and the Politics of Nineteenth Century US House Elections." *American Journal of Political Science* 50: 289.
77 Engstrom, *Partisan Gerrymandering and the Construction of American Democracy*, 171.
78 Ibid., 172–3.
79 Key, V. O., Jr. 1958. *Politics, Parties, and Pressure Groups*, 4th edn. New York: Thomas Y. Crowell Co., 318.
80 Engstrom, *Partisan Gerrymandering and the Construction of American Democracy*, 175 (figure 9.3).
81 Ibid., 174–5.
82 Eagles, Charles W. 1990. *Democracy Delayed: Congressional Reapportionment and Urban–Rural Conflict in the 1920s*. Athens, GA: University of Georgia Press.
83 Belknap, Michal R. 2005. *The Supreme Court Under Earl Warren, 1953–1969*. Columbia, SC: University of South Carolina Press, 111.

84 Ansolabehere, Stephen and James M. Snyder, Jr. 2008. *The End of Inequality: One Person, One Vote and the Transformation of American Politics.* New York: W.W. Norton & Company, 54.
85 Ibid.
86 Ibid., 54–5.

CHAPTER 3. THE LEGAL STATUS OF GERRYMANDERING

1 Ansolabehere, Stephen and James M. Snyder, Jr. 2008. *The End of Inequality: One Person, One Vote and the Transformation of American Politics.* New York: W.W. Norton & Company, 95.
2 Smith, J. Douglas. 2014. *On Democracy's Doorstep: The Inside Story of How the Supreme Court Brought 'One Person, One Vote' to the United States.* New York: Hill and Wang, 58; 54.
3 Ibid., 60.
4 *Colegrove v. Green,* 328 U.S. 549 (1946).
5 As quoted in Ansolabehere and Snyder, *The End of Inequality,* 103.
6 Ibid., 105.
7 As quoted in Smith, *On Democracy's Doorstep,* 62.
8 *Baker v. Carr,* 369 U.S. 186 (1962).
9 Smith, *On Democracy's Doorstep,* 72–5.
10 Ibid., 80.
11 As quoted in ibid., 82.
12 Ibid., 85.
13 Ibid., 89–91.
14 Cortner, Richard C. 1970. *The Apportionment Cases.* Knoxville, TN: The University of Tennessee Press, 135.
15 As quoted in ibid.
16 Ansolabehere and Snyder, *The End of Inequality,* 164–5.
17 *Gray v. Sanders,* 372 U.S. 368 (1963).
18 Ansolabehere and Snyder, *The End of Inequality,* 165.
19 As quoted in ibid., 166.
20 *Wesberry v. Sanders,* 376 U.S. 1 (1964); *Reynolds v. Sims,* 377 U.S. 533 (1964).
21 As quoted in Smith, *On Democracy's Doorstep,* 197.
22 As quoted in ibid., 214.

23 *Lucas v. Forty-Fourth General Assembly of Colorado*, 377 U.S. 713 (1964).
24 As quoted in Smith, *On Democracy's Doorstep*, 214–15.
25 Cortner, *The Apportionment Cases*, 230. On the federal analogy, see also McKay, Robert B. 1963. "The Federal Analogy and State Apportionment Standards." *Notre Dame Law Review* 38: 487–98.
26 As quoted in Cortner, *The Apportionment Cases*, 230.
27 Ansolabehere and Snyder, *The End of Inequality*, 178.
28 *Gaffney v. Cummings*, 412 U.S. 735 (1973).
29 National Conference of State Legislatures. 2019. "Redistricting and the Supreme Court: The Most Significant Cases." April 25. http://www.ncsl.org/research/redistricting/redistricting-and-the-supreme-court-the-most-significant-cases.aspx (accessed December 20, 2019).
30 *Gaffney v. Cummings*, 412 U.S. 735 (1973) at 777.
31 *Karcher v. Daggett*, 462 U.S. 725 (1983).
32 National Conference of State Legislatures, "Redistricting and the Supreme Court."
33 *Evenwel v. Abbott*, 136 S. Ct. 1120 (2016).
34 See Denniston, Lyle. 2016. "Opinion analysis: Leaving a constitutional ideal still undefined." SCOTUSblog, April 4. https://www.scotusblog.com/2016/04/opinion-analysis-leaving-a-constitutional-ideal-still-undefined/ (accessed December 20, 2019).
35 Fishkin, Joseph. 2019. "The Evenwel Gambit." Balkinization, July 6. https://balkin.blogspot.com/2019/07/the-evenwel-gambit.html (accessed December 20, 2019). See also Hasen, Rick. 2019. "If Trump's Executive Order Ends Up Creating Better Citizenship Data, Could It Be Used by States to Draw CONGRESSIONAL Districts with Equal Numbers of Voter Eligible Persons (and Not Total Population)? Would It Allow for Use in State and Local Districts?" Election Law Blog, July 12. https://electionlawblog.org/?p=106205 (accessed December 20, 2019).
36 *Gomillion v. Lightfoot*, 364 U.S. 339 (1960).
37 Smith, *On Democracy's Doorstep*, 65.
38 Ibid., 66.
39 See key provisions of the Voting Rights Act at https://avalon.law.yale.edu/20th_century/voting_rights_1965.asp (accessed December 20, 2019).
40 *City of Mobile v. Bolden*, 446 U.S. 55 (1980).

41 Bullock, Charles S. III. 2010. *Redistricting: The Most Political Activity in America*. Lanham, MD: Rowman & Littlefield, 57–9.
42 *Thornburg v. Gingles*, 478 U.S. 30 (1986).
43 Scher, Richard K., Jon L. Mills, and John J. Hotaling. 1997. *Voting Rights & Democracy: The Law and Politics of Districting*. Chicago, IL: Nelson-Hall Publishers, 76.
44 As quoted in Scher, Mills, and Hotaling, *Voting Rights & Democracy*, 78.
45 See ibid., 78–85.
46 Ibid., 84.
47 *Shaw v. Reno*, 509 U.S. 630 (1993).
48 As quoted in Scher, Mills, and Hotaling, *Voting Rights & Democracy*, 94.
49 Ibid., 94–7.
50 *Miller v. Johnson*, 515 U.S. 900 (1995).
51 Scher, Mills, and Hotaling, *Voting Rights & Democracy*, 100–11.
52 *Bush v. Vera*, 517 U.S. 952 (1996).
53 *Shaw v. Hunt*, 517 U.S. 899 (1996), often referred to as *Shaw II*, at 907.
54 Ebaugh, Nelson. 1997. "Refining the Racial Gerrymandering Claim: Bush v. Vera." *Tulsa Law Review* 33: 613–41.
55 *Easley v. Cromartie*, 532 U.S. 234 (2001).
56 Ibid., 243.
57 Lowenstein, Daniel Hays and Richard L. Hasen. 2004. *Election Law: Cases and Materials*, 3rd edn. Durham, NC: Carolina Academic Press, 316.
58 *Shelby County v. Holder*, 570 U.S. 529 (2013).
59 See Engstrom, Richard L. 2014. "*Shelby County v. Holder* and the Gutting of Federal Preclearance of Election Law Changes." *Politics, Groups, and Identities* 2: 530–48.
60 Brennan Center for Justice. 2018. "How We Can Restore the Voting Rights Act." BrennanCenter.org, August 6. https://www.brennancenter.org/our-work/research-reports/how-we-can-restore-voting-rights-act (accessed December 27, 2019). See also Katz, Ellen D. 2018. "Section 2 After Section 5: Voting Rights and the Race to the Bottom." *William & Mary Law Review* 59: 1961–91.
61 Hasen, Richard L. 2016–2017. "Resurrection: *Cooper v. Harris* and the Transformation of Racial Gerrymandering into a Voting Rights Tool." *ACS Supreme Court Review* 1: 113.

62 *Cooper v. Harris*, 137 S. Ct. 1455 (2017).

63 Hasen, "Resurrection," 116–17.

64 Ibid., 117.

65 As quoted in ibid., 125.

66 Hasen, Richard L. 2018. "Race or Party, Race as Party, or Party All the Time: Three Uneasy Approaches to Conjoined Polarization in Redistricting and Voting Cases." *William & Mary Law Review* 59: 1837–86.

67 Ibid.

68 Baker, Gordon E. 1990. "The Unfinished Reapportionment Revolution." In *Political Gerrymandering and the Courts*, ed. Bernard Grofman. New York: Agathon Press, 18.

69 Quoted in ibid., 18–19 (emphasis mine).

70 Ibid., 19.

71 *Davis v. Bandemer*, 478 U.S. 109 (1986).

72 See, for example, Lowenstein and Hasen, *Election Law*, 3rd edn, 329–30.

73 Bullock, *Redistricting*, 129.

74 Justice White's plurality opinion as quoted in Frient, Megan Creek. 1998. "Similar Harm Means Similar Claims: Doing Away with *Davis v. Bandemer's* Discriminatory Effect Requirement in Political Gerrymandering Cases." *Case Western Law Review* 48: 635.

75 Hasen, Richard L. 2005. "Looking for Standards (in All the Wrong Places): Partisan Gerrymandering Claims after *Veith*." *Election Law Journal* 3: 626 (quoting Justice White's *Bandemer* opinion).

76 See, for example, Grofman, Bernard. 1983. "Measures of Bias and Proportionality in Seats–Votes Relationships." *Political Methodology* 9: 295–327.

77 Grofman, Bernard. 1990. "Toward a Coherent Theory of Gerrymandering: *Bandemer* and *Thornburg*." In *Political Gerrymandering and the Courts*, ed. Bernard Grofman. New York: Agathon Press, 44.

78 Ibid.

79 Ibid., 45.

80 Bullock, *Redistricting*, 122, table 5.4.

81 *Vieth v. Jubelirer*, 541 U.S. 267 (2004).

82 Weaver, Michael. 2005. "Uncertainty Maintained: The Split Decision over Partisan Gerrymanders in *Vieth v. Jubelirer*." *Loyola University Chicago Law Journal* 36: 1313–26.

83 Lowenstein, Daniel Hays, Richard L. Hasen, Daniel P. Tokaji, and Nicholas Stephanopoulos. 2017. *Election Law: Cases and Materials*, 6th edn. Durham, NC: Carolina Academic Press, 185.
84 Ibid.
85 Though see Lowenstein, Daniel H. 2005. "*Vieth's* Gap: Has the Supreme Court Gone from Bad to Worse on Partisan Gerrymandering?" *Cornell Journal of Law and Public Policy* 14: 367–95. Lowenstein argues that, because *Vieth* did not establish a new standard, nor overturn *Bandemer*, the *Bandemer* standard was still in effect following *Vieth*.
86 Hasen, "Looking for Standards (in All the Wrong Places)."
87 Gardner, James A. 2004. "A Post-*Vieth* Strategy for Litigating Partisan Gerrymandering Claims." *Election Law Journal* 3: 643–52.
88 Pugh, Amy M. 2005. "Unresolved: Whether a Claim for Political Gerrymandering May be Brought Under the First Amendment?" *Northern Kentucky Law Review* 32: 373–96; and Caum, Timothy D., II. 2005. "Partisan Gerrymandering Challenges in Light of *Vieth v. Jubelirer*: A First Amendment Alternative." *Temple Political & Civil Rights Law Review* 15: 287–322.
89 *League of United Latin American Citizens v. Perry*, 548 U.S. 399 (2006).
90 Lowenstein, Hasen, Tokaji, and Stephanopoulos, *Election Law*, 6th edn, 187–94.
91 The key pieces of scholarship in this body of work are King, Gary and Robert X. Browning. 1987. "Democratic Representation and Partisan Bias in Congressional Elections." *American Political Science Review* 81: 1251–73; King, Gary. 1989. "Representation through Legislative Redistricting: A Stochastic Model." *American Journal of Political Science* 33: 787–824; Gelman, Andrew and Gary King. 1994. "Enhancing Democracy through Legislative Redistricting." *American Political Science Review* 88: 541–59; and Gelman, Andrew and Gary King. 1994. "A Unified Method of Evaluating Electoral Systems and Redistricting Plans." *American Journal of Political Science* 38: 514–54.
92 King, Gary, Bernard Grofman, Andrew Gelman, and Jonathan Katz. 2005. "Brief of *Amicus Curiae*, in Support of Neither Party, in *LULAC v. Perry*, 4–5, https://gking.harvard.edu/files/gking/files/amicus-sym_01.pdf (accessed December 30, 2019).

93 Ibid., 9 (emphasis in original).
94 Justice Stevens' dissenting opinion as quoted in Grofman, Bernard and Gary King. 2007. "The Future of Partisan Symmetry as a Judicial Test for Partisan Gerrymandering after *LULAC v. Perry*." *Election Law Journal* 6: 4.
95 Justice Kennedy's opinion in *LULAC* as quoted in ibid. (emphasis added).
96 *Gill v. Whitford*, No. 16-1161 (2018).
97 Stephanopoulos, Nicholas O. and Eric M. McGhee. 2015. "Partisan Gerrymandering and the Efficiency Gap." *The University of Chicago Law Review* 82: 850.
98 Ibid., 851. See also McGhee, Eric. 2014. "Measuring Partisan Bias in Single-Member District Electoral Systems." *Legislative Studies Quarterly* 39: 55–85; and McGhee, Eric. 2017. "Measuring Efficiency in Redistricting." *Election Law Journal* 16: 1–26.
99 Trende, Sean. 2019. "What's Wrong with the Efficiency Gap?" American Enterprise Institute, June. https://www.aei.org/wp-content/uploads/2019/06/Whats-Wrong-With-The-Efficiency-Gap.pdf (accessed December 30, 2019); Chambers, Christopher P., Alan D. Miller, and Joel Sobel. 2017. "Flaws in the Efficiency Gap." *Journal of Law & Politics* 33: 1–33; and Cover, Benjamin Plener. 2018. "Quantifying Partisan Gerrymandering: An Evaluation of the Efficiency Gap Proposal." *Stanford Law Review* 70: 1131–232.
100 See McGann, Anthony J., Charles Anthony Smith, Michael Latner, and Alex Keena. 2016. *Gerrymandering in America: The House of Representatives, the Supreme Court, and the Future of Popular Sovereignty*. New York: Cambridge University Press, 69; and Goedert, Nicholas. 2015. "Use of Efficiency Gap in Analyzing Partisan Gerrymandering." Report for the State of Wisconsin, *Whitford v. Nichol*. https://campaignlegal.org/sites/default/files/1%2BNicholas%2BGoedert%2BExpert%2BReport%2B%28Dkt.%2B51%29.pdf (accessed December 30, 2019).
101 McDonald, Michael D. and Robin E. Best. 2015. "Unfair Partisan Gerrymanders in Politics and Law: A Diagnostic Applied to Six Cases." *Election Law Journal* 14: 312–30.
102 Cho, Wendy K. Tam and Yan Y. Liu. 2016. "Toward a Talismanic Redistricting Tool: A Computational Method for Identifying Extreme Redistricting Plans." *Election Law Journal* 15: 351–66.
103 *Rucho v. Common Cause*, 588 U.S. ___ (2019).

104 Justice Roberts' opinion in ibid. (slip op. at 30).
105 Justice Kagan's dissent in ibid. (slip op. at 32 and 33).
106 See Hasen, Richard L. 2019. "The Gerrymandering Decision Drags the Supreme Court Further into the Mud." *The New York Times*, June 27. https://www.nytimes.com/2019/06/27/opinion/gerrymand ering-rucho-supreme-court.html (accessed May 22, 2019).

CHAPTER 4. HOW GERRYMANDERING WORKS

1 See National Conference of State Legislatures. 2018. "The 'Iowa Model' for Redistricting." NCSL.org, April 6. https://www.ncsl. org/research/redistricting/the-iowa-model-for-redistricting.aspx (accessed January 7, 2020).
2 National Conference of State Legislatures. 2019. "Redistricting Commissions: Congressional Plans." NCSL.org, April 18. https:// www.ncsl.org/research/redistricting/redistricting-commissions-con gressional-plans.aspx#Primary (accessed January 8, 2020).
3 National Conference of State Legislatures. 2019. "Redistricting Commissions: State Legislative Plans." NCSL.org, April 18. https:// www.ncsl.org/research/redistricting/2009-redistricting-commis sions-table.aspx#Commissions%20with%20Primary%20Respon sibility (accessed January 7, 2020).
4 Cain, Bruce E. 2012. "Redistricting Commissions: A Better Political Buffer." *Yale Law Journal* 121: 1816.
5 Ibid., 1817.
6 Levitt, Justin. 2010. "A Citizen's Guide to Redistricting." Brennan Center for Justice, 45. https://www.brennancenter.org/sites/default/ files/2019-08/Report_CGR-2010-edition.pdf (accessed January 17, 2020).
7 Ibid., 46.
8 Ballotpedia. N.d. "State legislative chambers that use multi-member districts." Ballotpedia.org. https://ballotpedia.org/State_legislative_ chambers_that_use_multi-member_districts (accessed January 17, 2020).
9 See National Conference of State Legislatures. 2009. "Redistricting Law 2010." NCSL.org, November, 109. https://www.ncsl.org/Por tals/1/Documents/Redistricting/Redistricting_2010.pdf (accessed January 14, 2020).

10 Altman, Micah and Michael P. McDonald. 2012. "Redistricting Principles for the Twenty-First Century." *Case Western Reserve Law Review* 62: 1190.
11 Chambers, Christopher P. and Alan D. Miller. 2013. "Measuring Legislative Boundaries." *Mathematical Social Sciences* 66: 268.
12 Ibid.
13 Reock, Ernest C. 1961. "A Note: Measuring Compactness as a Requirement of Legislative Apportionment." *Midwest Journal of Political Science* 5: 70–4.
14 Harris, Curtis C. 1964. "A Scientific Method of Districting." *Behavioral Science* 9: 219–25.
15 Chambers and Miller, "Measuring Legislative Boundaries," 269.
16 Polsby, Daniel D. and Robert D. Popper. 1991. "The Third Criterion: Compactness as a Procedural Safeguard Against Partisan Gerrymandering." *Yale Law and Policy Review* 9: 301–53.
17 Schwartzberg, Joseph E. 1965. "Reapportionment, Gerrymanders, and the Notion of 'Compactness'." *Minnesota Law Review* 50: 443–52.
18 Chambers and Miller, "Measuring Legislative Boundaries," 269.
19 Kaufman, Aaron, Gary King, and Mayya Komisarchik. Forthcoming. "How to Measure Legislative District Compactness If You Only Know it When you See it." *American Journal of Political Science*, 6. https://gking.harvard.edu/files/gking/files/compact.pdf (last accessed December 29, 2020).
20 Levitt, "A Citizen's Guide to Redistricting," 50.
21 Ibid.
22 Ibid., 54.
23 Ibid.
24 Ibid.
25 Stephanopoulos, Nicholas O. 2012. "Redistricting and the Territorial Community." *University of Pennsylvania Law Review* 160: 1391. It should be noted that Stephanopoulos does not think territorial communities are necessarily congruent with political subdivisions, nor does he think they are synonymous with "communities of interest" (see discussion below); ibid., 1385.
26 Levitt, "A Citizen's Guide to Redistricting," 56.
27 See the discussion of "outcome-based regulations" in Altman and McDonald, "Redistricting Principles for the Twenty-First Century," 1190–2.

28 Due to the COVID-19 pandemic, the Census Bureau requested a revised delivery date for these data of July 31, 2021. As of this writing, Congress had not approved the extension. See https://2020 census.gov/en/news-events/operational-adjustments-covid-19.html (accessed May 25, 2020).

29 Cho, Wendy K. Tam and Yan Y. Liu. 2016. "Toward a Talismanic Redistricting Tool: A Computation Method for Identifying Extreme Redistricting Plans." *Election Law Journal* 15: 357.

30 See United States Census Bureau. N.d. "Introduction to Geographies Tutorial." https://data.census.gov/cedsci/webpages?q=Introduction %20to%20Geographies%20Tutorial (accessed October 18, 2020).

31 Wattson, Peter S. 2011. "How to Draw Redistricting Plans That Will Stand Up in Court." National Conference of State Legislatures, January 22, 9–10. https://www.ncsl.org/documents/legismgt/How_To_Draw_Maps.pdf (accessed December 19, 2019).

32 United States Government Accountability Office. 2018. "2020 Census: Actions Needed to Address Challenges to Enumerating Hard-to-Count Groups." GAO-18-599, 6. https://www.gao.gov/assets/700/693450.pdf (accessed February 9, 2020).

33 Ibid., 4.

34 *Department of Commerce v. United States House of Representatives*, 525 U.S. 316 (1999).

35 Liptak, Adam. 2019. "Supreme Court Leaves Census Question on Citizenship in Doubt." *The New York Times*, June 27. https://www.nytimes.com/2019/06/27/us/politics/census-citizenship-question-supreme-court.html (accessed February 4, 2020). For more on *Department of Commerce v. New York*, see Oyez.org. N.d., "Department of Commerce v. New York," https://www.oyez.org/cases/2018/18-966 (accessed February 4, 2020).

36 Wines, Michael. 2019. "A Census Whodunit: Why Was the Citizenship Question Added?" *The New York Times*, November 30, updated December 2. https://www.nytimes.com/2019/11/30/us/census-citizenship-question-hofeller.html (accessed February 4, 2020).

37 Wines, Michael. 2019. "Deceased G.O.P. Strategist's Hard Drives Reveal New Details on the Census Citizenship Question." *The New York Times*, May 30. https://www.nytimes.com/2019/05/30/us/census-citizenship-question-hofeller.html (accessed February 4, 2020).

38 Lowenstein, Daniel Hays, Richard L. Hasen, Daniel P. Tokaji, and Nicholas Stephanopoulos. 2017. *Election Law: Cases and Materials*, 6th edn. Durham, NC: Carolina Academic Press, 100. For more on *Evenwel v. Abbott*, see Oyez.org. N.d. "Evenwel v. Abbott," https://www.oyez.org/cases/2015/14-940 (accessed February 4, 2020).

39 See Hasen, Rick. 2019. "The Evenwel Gambit." Election Law Blog, July 6. https://electionlawblog.org/?p=106098 (accessed February 4, 2020).

40 The National Conference of State Legislatures compiles a list of vendors who offer redistricting software, which can be found at https://www.ncsl.org/research/redistricting/redistricting-vendors.aspx (accessed February 12).

41 Vickrey, William. 1961. "On the Prevention of Gerrymandering." *Political Science Quarterly* 76: 105–10; Weaver, James B. and Sidney W. Hess. 1963. "A Procedure for Nonpartisan Districting: Development of Computer Techniques." *Yale Law Journal* 73: 288–309; and Hess, S.W., J.B. Weaver, H.J. Siegfeldt, J.N. Whelan, and P.A. Zitlau. 1965. "Nonpartisan Political Redistricting by Computer." *Operations Research* 13: 998–1006.

42 Altman, Micah, Karin Mac Donald, and Michael McDonald. 2005. "From Crayons to Computers: The Evolution of Computer Use in Redistricting." *Social Science Computer Review* 23: 335.

43 Ibid., 336.

44 Ibid., 337.

45 Ibid., 342.

46 Altman, Micah, Karin Mac Donald, and Michael McDonald. 2005. "Pushbutton Gerrymanders? How Computing Has Changed Redistricting." In *Party Lines: Competition, Partisanship, and Congressional Redistricting*, eds. Thomas E. Mann and Bruce E. Cain. Washington, DC: Brookings Institution Press, 58. See also Altman, Micah and Michael McDonald. 2010. "The Promise and Perils of Computers in Redistricting." *Duke Journal of Constitutional Law & Public Policy* 5: 69–111.

47 Altman, Mac Donald, and McDonald, "Pushbutton Gerrymanders?," 58.

48 Altman, Mac Donald, and McDonald, "From Crayons to Computers," 343.

49 Ibid.

50 Altman, Mac Donald, and McDonald, "Pushbutton Gerrymanders?," 61.
51 Altman, Mac Donald, and McDonald, "From Crayons to Computers," 343.
52 Altman, Mac Donald, and McDonald, "Pushbutton Gerrymanders?," 58–9; 62.
53 Altman, Mac Donald, and McDonald, "From Crayons to Computers," 343.
54 McDonald, Michael and Micah Altman. 2018. *The Public Mapping Project: How Public Participation Can Revolutionize Redistricting.* Ithaca, NY: Cornell University Press, 18.
55 Ibid., 26–7.
56 Ibid.
57 Ibid., 27.
58 Ibid.
59 See McDonald and Altman, *The Public Mapping Project.* The Public Mapping Project website is http://www.publicmapping.org/ (last accessed February 23, 2020).
60 Ibid., 37.
61 Vickrey, "On the Prevention of Gerrymandering." More recently, see Browdy, Michelle H. 1989–1990. "Computer Models and Post-Bandemer Redistricting." *Yale Law Journal* 99: 1379–98.
62 Altman and McDonald. "The Promise and Perils of Computers in Redistricting."
63 McDonald and Altman, *The Public Mapping Project,* 51.
64 Ibid., 66.
65 Altman, Micah. 1997. "The Computational Complexity of Automated Redistricting: Is Automation the Answer?" *Rutgers Computer & Technology Law Journal* 23: 88–94.
66 Ibid., 95.
67 Ibid., 97.
68 Levitt, "A Citizen's Guide to Redistricting," 57.
69 Niemi, Richard G. and John Deegan, Jr. 1978. "A Theory of Political Districting." *American Political Science Review* 72: 1305.
70 Cain, Bruce E., Karin Mac Donald, and Iris Hui. 2006. "Competition and Redistricting in California: Lessons for Reform." Institute of Governmental Studies, University of California at Berkeley. https://statewidedatabase.org/resources/redistricting_research/Competition_&_Redistricting.pdf (accessed February 27, 2020).

71 They use races for California lieutenant governor, secretary of state, attorney general, controller, treasurer, and insurance commissioner. Ibid., 32.
72 Ibid.
73 Bishop, Bill. 2009. *The Big Sort: Why the Clustering of Like-Minded America is Tearing Us Apart.* New York: Mariner Books.
74 McDonald, Michael P. 2006. "Redistricting and Competitive Districts." In *The Marketplace of Democracy: Electoral Competition and American Politics*, eds. Michael P. McDonald and John Samples. Washington, DC: Brookings Institution Press, 222.
75 Ibid., 240.
76 Bullock, Charles S. III. 2010. *Redistricting: The Most Political Activity in America.* Lanham, MD: Rowman & Littlefield, 123.
77 Levitt, "A Citizen's Guide to Redistricting," 61.
78 See Bullock, *Redistricting*, 124–5.
79 Figures were created for the author by Colin Medvic.
80 Levitt, "A Citizen's Guide to Redistricting," 58.
81 McGann, Anthony J., Charles Anthony Smith, Michael Latner, and Alex Keena. 2016. *Gerrymandering in America: The House of Representatives, the Supreme Court, and the Future of Popular Sovereignty.* New York: Cambridge University Press, 57.

CHAPTER 5. THE CONSEQUENCES OF GERRYMANDERING

1 Severns, Maggie. 2020. "Democrats plan $50M campaign to flip state legislatures before redistricting." *Politico*, January 15. https://www.politico.com/news/2020/01/15/redistricting-state-legislatures-campaign-099437 (accessed March 5, 2020); and Brower, Pieter. 2020. "ICYMI: DLCC Launches Flip Everything Campaign." Democratic Legislative Campaign Committee, January 17. https://www.dlcc.org/press/icymi-dlcc-launches-flip-everything-campaign (accessed March 5, 2020).
2 National Democratic Redistricting Committee. N.d. "About the NDRC." https://democraticredistricting.com/about/ (accessed March 5, 2020).

3 Republican State Leadership Committee. 2015. "RSLC Launches REDMAP 2020, Sets $125 Million Investment Goal." July 16. https://sglf.org/2015/07/16/rslc-launches-redmap-2020-sets-125-million-investment-goal/ (accessed October 18, 2020).
4 Republican State Leadership Committee. 2019. "RSLC Launches Major Redistricting Initiative for 2019–2020 Election Cycle." September 5. https://rslc.gop/rslc-launches-major-redistricting-initiative/ (accessed October 18, 2020).
5 National Republican Redistricting Trust. N.d. "About us." https://www.thenrrt.org/about-us/ (accessed March 5, 2020).
6 Tufte, Edward R. 1973. "The Relationship between Seats and Votes in Two-Party Systems." *American Political Science Review* 57: 553.
7 McDonald, Michael P. 2006. "Drawing the Line on District Competition." *PS: Political Science and Politics* 39: 91–4; McDonald, Michael P. 2006. "Re-Drawing the Line on District Competition." *PS: Political Science and Politics* 39: 99–101; and Altman, Micah and Michael McDonald. 2015. "Redistricting and Polarization." In *American Gridlock: The Sources, Character, and Impact of Political Polarization*, eds. James A. Thurber and Antoine Yoshinaka. New York: Cambridge University Press. See also Cain, Bruce E., Karin Mac Donald, and Michael McDonald. 2005. "From Equality to Fairness: The Path of Political Reform since *Baker v. Carr*." In *Party Lines: Competition, Partisanship, and Congressional Redistricting*, eds. Thomas E. Mann and Bruce E. Cain. Washington, DC: Brookings Institution Press; and Lublin, David and Michael P. McDonald. 2006. "Is It Time to Draw the Line?: The Impact of Redistricting on Competition in State House Elections." *Election Law Journal*, 5: 144–57.
8 Abramowitz, Alan I., Brad Alexander, and Matthew Gunning. 2006. "Incumbency, Redistricting, and the Decline of Competition in U.S. House Elections." *The Journal of Politics*, 68: 79. See also Abramowitz, Alan, Brad Alexander, and Matthew Gunning. 2006. "Don't Blame Redistricting for Uncompetitive Elections." *PS: Political Science and Politics* 39: 87–90; and Abramowitz, Alan, Brad Alexander, and Matthew Gunning. 2006. "Drawing the Line on District Competition: A Rejoinder." *PS: Political Science and Politics* 39: 95–7.
9 McDonald, "Drawing the Line on District Competition," 91.

10 Ibid.
11 Stephanopoulos, Nicholas O. and Christopher Warshaw. 2020. "The Impact of Partisan Gerrymandering on Political Parties." *Legislative Studies Quarterly*, https://doi.org/10.1111/lsq.12276.
12 See, for example, Bullock, Charles S. 1975. "Redistricting and Congressional Stability, 1962–72." *The Journal of Politics* 37: 569–75.
13 Goedert, Nicholas. 2017. "The Pseudoparadox of Partisan Mapmaking and Congressional Competition." *State Politics & Policy Quarterly* 17: 48.
14 Ibid., 54.
15 Masket, Seth E., Jonathan Winburn, and Gerald C. Wright. 2012. "The Gerrymanderers Are Coming! Legislative Redistricting Won't Affect Competition or Polarization Much, No Matter Who Does It." *PS: Political Science & Politics* 45: 39–43.
16 Hetherington, Marc J., Bruce Larson, and Suzanne Globetti. 2003. "The Redistricting Cycle and Strategic Candidate Decisions in U.S. House Races." *The Journal of Politics* 65: 1221–34.
17 Ibid., 1232.
18 Seabrook, Nicholas R. 2017. *Drawing the Lines: Constraints on Partisan Gerrymandering in U.S. Politics*. Ithaca, NY: Cornell University Press, 115.
19 Henderson, John A., Brian T. Hamel, and Aaron M. Goldzimer. 2018. "Gerrymandering Incumbency: Does Nonpartisan Redistricting Increase Electoral Competition?" *The Journal of Politics* 80: 1015.
20 Masket, Winburn, and Wright, "The Gerrymanderers Are Coming!," 41.
21 Ibid., 43.
22 Carson, Jamie L. and Michael H. Crespin. 2004. "The Effect of State Redistricting Methods on Electoral Competition in United States House of Representatives Races." *State Politics & Policy Quarterly* 4: 455–69.
23 Carson, Jamie L., Michael H. Crespin, and Ryan D. Williamson. 2014. "Reevaluating the Effects of Redistricting on Electoral Competition, 1972–2012." *State Politics & Policy Quarterly* 14: 174.
24 Lindgren, Eric and Priscilla Southwell. 2013. "The Effect of Redistricting Commissions on Electoral Competitiveness in

U.S. House Elections, 2002–2010." *Journal of Politics and Law* 6: 13–18.

25 Goedert, "The Pseudoparadox of Partisan Mapmaking."

26 Williamson, Ryan D. 2019. "Examining the Effects of Partisan Redistricting on Candidate Entry Decisions." *Election Law Journal* 18: 222.

27 Seabrook, *Drawing the Lines*, 108–9.

28 Ibid., 111.

29 Erikson, Robert S. 1972. "Malapportionment, Gerrymandering, and Party Fortunes in Congressional Elections." *American Political Science Review* 66: 1234–45.

30 Ibid., 1244.

31 Ibid.

32 Cox, Gary W. and Jonathan N. Katz. 1999. "The Reapportionment Revolution and Bias in U.S. Congressional Elections." *American Journal of Political Science* 43: 834. See also Cox, Gary W. and Jonathan N. Katz. 2002. *Elbridge Gerry's Salamander: The Electoral Consequences of the Reapportionment Revolution.* New York: Cambridge University Press.

33 Cox and Katz, "The Reapportionment Revolution," 834.

34 Cain, Bruce E. 1985. "Assessing the Partisan Effects of Redistricting." *American Political Science Review* 79: 320–33; and Gopoian, J. David and Darrell M. West. 1984. "Trading Security for Seats: Strategic Considerations in the Redistricting Process." *The Journal of Politics* 46: 1080–96.

35 Gopoian and West, "Trading Security for Seats," 1090.

36 Niemi, Richard G. and Laura R. Winsky. 1992. "The Persistence of Partisan Redistricting Effects in Congressional Elections in the 1970s and 1980s." *The Journal of Politics*, 54: 571.

37 Campagna, Janet and Bernard Grofman. 1990. "Party Control and Partisan Bias in 1980s Congressional Redistricting." *The Journal of Politics* 52: 1242–57.

38 Born, Richard. 1985. "Partisan Intentions and Election Day Realities in the Congressional Redistricting Process." *American Political Science Review* 79: 305.

39 Glazer, Amihai, Bernard Grofman, and Marc Robbins. 1987. "Partisan and Incumbency Effects of 1970s Congressional Redistricting." *American Journal of Political Science*, 31: 701.

40 Scarrow, Howard A. 1982. "Partisan Gerrymandering – Invidious

or Benevolent? *Gaffney v. Cummings* and Its Aftermath." *The Journal of Politics* 44: 820.

41 Niemi, Richard G. and Simon Jackman. 1991. "Bias and Responsiveness in State Legislative Districting." *Legislative Studies Quarterly* 16: 198.

42 Ibid.

43 Basehart, Harry and John Comer. 1991. "Partisan and Incumbent Effects in State Legislative Redistricting." *Legislative Studies Quarterly* 16: 75.

44 Gelman, Andrew and Gary King. 1994. "Enhancing Democracy Through Legislative Redistricting." *American Political Science Review* 88: 550–2.

45 Ibid., 551.

46 Ibid., 551–2.

47 Niemi, Richard G. and Alan I. Abramowitz. 1994. "Partisan Redistricting and the 1992 Congressional Elections." *The Journal of Politics* 56: 815.

48 Swain, John W., Stephen A. Borrelli, and Brian C. Reed. 1998. "Partisan Consequences of the Post-1990 Redistricting for the U.S. House of Representatives." *Political Research Quarterly* 51: 961.

49 Ibid.

50 Petrocik, John R. and Scott W. Desposato. 1998. "The Partisan Consequences of Majority-Minority Redistricting in the South, 1992 and 1994." *The Journal of Politics* 60: 630, emphasis in original.

51 Seabrook, Nicholas R. 2010. "The Limits of Partisan Gerrymandering: Looking Ahead to the 2010 Congressional Redistricting Cycle." *The Forum* 8: Article 8, 8.

52 Ibid., 11.

53 Grofman, Bernard and Thomas L. Brunell. 2005. "The Art of the Dummymander: The Impact of Recent Redistrictings on the Partisan Makeup of Southern House Seats." In *Redistricting in the New Millennium*, ed. Peter F. Galderisi. Lanham, MD: Lexington Books. See also Goedert, "The Pseudoparadox of Partisan Mapmaking and Congressional Competition."

54 McCarty, Nolan, Keith T. Poole, and Howard Rosenthal. 2009. "Does Gerrymandering Cause Polarization?" *American Journal of Political Science* 53: 678.

55 Arbour, Brian K. and Seth C. McKee. 2005–6. "Cracking Back: The Effectiveness of Partisan Redistricting in the Texas House of Representatives." *The American Review of Politics* 26: 397.

56 Ibid.

57 As quoted in McKee, Seth C., Jeremy M. Teigen, and Mathieu Turgeon. 2006. "The Partisan Impact of Congressional Redistricting: The Case of Texas, 2001–2003." *Social Science Quarterly* 87: 309.

58 Ibid., 309–10.

59 Ibid., 313.

60 Goedert, Nicholas. 2014. "Gerrymandering or Geography? How Democrats Won the Popular Vote but Lost the Congress in 2012." *Research and Politics* 1, 1: 7.

61 Goedert, Nicholas. 2015. "The Case of the Disappearing Bias: A 2014 Update to the 'Gerrymandering or Geography' Debate." *Research and Politics* 2, 4: 5.

62 Ibid.

63 Engstrom, Richard L. 2020. "Partisan Gerrymandering: Weeds in the Political Thicket." *Social Science Quarterly* 101: 27.

64 Ibid., see table 1.

65 Ibid., 30.

66 McGann, Anthony J., Charles Anthony Smith, Michael Latner, and Alex Keena. 2016. *Gerrymandering in America: The House of Representatives, the Supreme Court, and the Future of Popular Sovereignty*. New York: Cambridge University Press, 156.

67 Ibid., 157.

68 Ibid., 162.

69 Ibid., 162–3.

70 Stephanopoulos, Nicholas O. 2018. "The Causes and Consequences of Gerrymandering." *William & Mary Law Review* 59: 2115–58.

71 Ibid., 2131–2.

72 Ibid., 2132.

73 Chen, Jowei and David Cottrell. 2016. "Evaluating Partisan Gains from Congressional Gerrymandering: Using Computer Simulations to Estimate the Effect of Gerrymandering in the U.S. House." *Electoral Studies* 44: 331.

74 Ibid., 339.

75 Ibid., 340.

76 Chen, Jowei and Jonathan Rodden. 2013. "Unintentional

Gerrymandering: Political Geography and Electoral Bias in Legislatures." *Quarterly Journal of Political Science* 8: 265.

77 Cain, "Assessing the Partisan Effects of Redistricting," 331.

78 For the original identification of the "vanishing marginals," see Mayhew, David R. 1974. "Congressional Elections: The Case of the Vanishing Marginals." *Polity* 6: 295–317. For trends over the entire 60-year period, see Erikson, Robert S. 2015. "The Congressional Incumbency Advantage over Sixty Years: Measurement, Trends, and Implications." In *Governing in a Polarized Age: Elections, Parties, and Political Representation in America*, eds. Alan S. Gerber and Eric Schickler. New York: Cambridge University Press.

79 Ansolabehere, Stephen and James M. Snyder, Jr. 2002. "The Incumbency Advantage in U.S. Elections: An Analysis of State and Federal Offices, 1942–2000." *Election Law Journal* 1: 319–21.

80 Erikson, "The Congressional Incumbency Advantage over Sixty Years," 66.

81 Ibid., 66, n. 1.

82 Basehart and Comer, "Partisan and Incumbent Effects in State Legislative Redistricting," 77.

83 Henderson, Hamel, and Goldzimer, "Gerrymandering Incumbency," 1015.

84 Cottrill, James B. 2012. "The Effects of Non-Legislative Approaches to Redistricting on Competition in Congressional Elections." *Polity* 44: 50.

85 Friedman, John N. and Richard T. Holden. 2009. "The Rising Incumbent Reelection Rate: What's Gerrymandering Got to Do With It?" *The Journal of Politics* 71: 609 (emphasis in original).

86 Ansolabehere, Stephen, James M. Snyder, Jr., and Charles Stewart, III. 2000. "Old Voters, New Voters, and the Personal Vote: Using Redistricting to Measure the Incumbency Advantage." *American Journal of Political Science* 44: 17–34; M.V. Hood, III and Seth C. McKee. 2008. "Gerrymandering on Georgia's Mind: The Effects of Redistricting on Vote Choice in the 2006 Midterm Election." *Social Science Quarterly* 89: 60–77; and M.V. Hood, III and Seth C. McKee. 2012. "Unwelcome Constituents: Redistricting and Countervailing Partisan Tides." *State Politics & Policy Quarterly* 13: 203–24.

87 Hayes, Danny and Seth C. McKee. 2009. "The Participatory Effects of Redistricting." *American Journal of Political Science* 53:

1006–23; and M.V. Hood, III and Seth C. McKee. 2010. "Stranger Danger: Redistricting, Incumbent Recognition, and Vote Choice." *Social Science Quarterly* 91: 344–58.

88 McKee, Seth C. 2008. "Redistricting and Familiarity With U.S. House Candidates." *American Politics Research* 36: 962–79.

89 See Banducci, Susan A. and Jeffrey A. Karp. 1994. "Electoral Consequences of Scandal and Reapportionment in the 1992 House Elections." *American Politics Quarterly* 22: 3–26.

90 Yoshinaka, Antoine and Chad Murphy. 2011. "The Paradox of Redistricting: How Partisan Mapmakers Foster Competition but Disrupt Representation." *Political Research Quarterly* 64: 441.

91 Ibid., 443.

92 Desposato, Scott W. and John R. Petrocik. 2003. "The Variable Incumbency Advantage: New Voters, Redistricting, and the Personal Vote." *American Journal of Political Science* 47: 28.

93 Ibid.

94 Tufte, "The Relationship between Seats and Votes in Two-Party Systems," 551.

95 Lyons, Michael and Peter F. Galderisi. 1995. "Incumbency, Reapportionment, and U.S. House Redistricting." *Political Research Quarterly* 48: 857–71.

96 Ibid., 868.

97 Ibid.

98 Born, Richard. 2020. "Contextual Effects of Redistricting on Old and New Voters: Sometimes Newcomer Ignorance Can Mean Electoral Bliss for the Incumbent." *American Review of Politics* 37: 44.

99 Hayes and McKee, "The Participatory Effects of Redistricting."

100 Hayes, Danny and Seth C. McKee. 2012. "The Intersection of Redistricting, Race, and Participation." *American Journal of Political Science* 56: 115–30.

101 Fraga, Bernard L. 2015. "Redistricting and the Causal Impact of Race on Voter Turnout." *The Journal of Politics* 78: 20.

102 Ibid., 30.

103 Hunt, Charles R. 2018. "When Does Redistricting Matter? Changing Conditions and Their Effects on Voter Turnout." *Electoral Studies* 54: 134.

104 Winburn, Jonathan and Michael W. Wagner. 2010. "Carving Voters Out: Redistricting's Influence on Political Information,

Turnout, and Voting Behavior." *Political Research Quarterly* 63: 373–86.
105 Hood and McKee, "Stranger Danger."
106 McKee, Seth C. 2008. "The Effects of Redistricting on Voting Behavior in Incumbent U.S. House Elections, 1992–1994." *Political Research Quarterly* 61: 129.
107 Hood and McKee, "Gerrymandering on Georgia's Mind."
108 Rush, Mark E. 1993. *Does Redistricting Make a Difference? Partisan Representation and Electoral Behavior*. Baltimore, MD: The Johns Hopkins University Press, chapter 6; Rush, Mark E. 2000. "Redistricting and Partisan Fluidity: Do We Really Know a Gerrymander When We See One?" *Political Geography* 19: 249–60.
109 Rush "Redistricting and Partisan Fluidity," 259.
110 Ibid., 256; emphasis in original.
111 Born, "Contextual Effects of Redistricting on Old and New Voters."
112 Ibid., 44.
113 Stephanopoulos and Warshaw, "The Impact of Partisan Gerrymandering on Political Parties."
114 Ibid., 27.
115 The literature on polarization in the United States is large and growing. For an accessible, but thorough, introduction to the phenomenon, see McCarty, Nolan. 2019. *Polarization: What Everyone Needs to Know*. New York: Oxford University Press.
116 See, for instance, Noel, Hans. 2014. *Political Ideologies and Political Parties in America*. New York: Cambridge University Press, chapter 7.
117 This description conflates policy and ideological polarization for simplicity's sake. See McCarty, *Polarization*, 8–12, for finer distinctions.
118 Altman, Micah and Michael McDonald. 2015. "Redistricting and Polarization." In *American Gridlock: The Sources, Character, and Impact of Political Polarization*, eds. James A. Thurber and Antoine Yoshinaka. New York: Cambridge University Press.
119 For some evidence of this, see Boatright, Robert G. 2004. "Static Ambition in a Changing World: Legislators' Preparations for, and Responses to, Redistricting." *State Politics and Policy Quarterly* 4: 436–54.

120 Altman and McDonald, "Redistricting and Polarization," 48–9.
121 Carson, Jamie L., Michael H. Crespin, Charles J. Finocchiaro, and David W. Rohde. 2007. "Redistricting and Party Polarization in the U.S. House of Representatives." *American Politics Research* 35: 899.
122 Caughey, Devin, Chris Tausanovitch, and Christopher Warshaw. 2017. "Partisan Gerrymandering and the Political Process: Effects on Roll-Call Voting and State Policies." *Election Law Journal* 16: 465.
123 Ibid., 462–3.
124 Stephanopoulos, "The Causes and Consequences of Gerrymandering," 2120.
125 Hayes, Matthew, Matthew V. Hibbing, and Tracy Sulkin. 2010. "Redistricting, Responsiveness, and Issue Attention." *Legislative Studies Quarterly* 35: 110.
126 Crespin, Michael H. 2010. "Serving Two Masters: Redistricting and Voting in the U.S. House of Representatives." *Political Research Quarterly* 63: 855.
127 Theriault, Sean M. 2008. *Party Polarization in Congress*. New York: Cambridge University Press, 82.
128 Ibid., 83.
129 McCarty, *Polarization*, 105.
130 Ibid., 106–7.
131 Ibid., 101–2.
132 McCarty, Poole, and Rosenthal, "Does Gerrymandering Cause Polarization?"
133 Ibid., 667.
134 Ibid.
135 Abramowitz, Alan. 2011. *The Disappearing Center: Engaged Citizens, Polarization, and American Democracy*. New Haven, CT: Yale University Press, chapter 7.
136 Mann, Thomas E. 2006. "Polarizing the House of Representatives: How Much Does Gerrymandering Matter?" In *Red and Blue Nation? Characteristics and Causes of American's Polarized Politics*, eds. Pietro S. Nivola and David W. Brady. Washington, DC: Brookings Institution Press, 267.
137 Ibid., 274–80.
138 Ibid., 281.

139 Masket, Winburn, and Wright, "The Gerrymanderers Are Coming!," 42–3.
140 Ibid., 42.
141 Ibid., emphasis in original.

CHAPTER 6. REFORM PROPOSALS

1 Mann, Thomas E. 2006. "Polarizing the House of Representatives: How Much Does Gerrymandering Matter?" In *Red and Blue Nation? Characteristics and Causes of American's Polarized Politics*, eds. Pietro S. Nivola and David W. Brady. Washington, DC: Brookings Institution Press, 280.
2 Buchler, Justin. 2010. "The Inevitability of Gerrymandering: Winners and Losers Under Alternative Approaches to Redistricting." *Duke Journal of Constitutional Law & Public Policy* 5: 17–36.
3 Buchler, Justin. 2005. "Competition, Representation and Redistricting: The Case Against Competitive Congressional Districts." *Journal of Theoretical Politics* 17: 431–63; and Brunell, Thomas L. 2008. *Redistricting and Representation: Why Competitive Elections are Bad for America*. New York: Routledge.
4 See National Conference of State Legislatures. 2018. "The 'Iowa Model' for Redistricting." NCSL.org, April 6. https://www.ncsl.org/research/redistricting/the-iowa-model-for-redistricting.aspx (accessed July 7, 2020).
5 Legislative Services Agency. 2007. "Legislative Guide to Redistricting in Iowa." https://www.legis.iowa.gov/docs/publications/LG/9461.pdf, 13–14 (accessed July 7, 2020).
6 National Conference of State Legislatures, "The 'Iowa Model' for Redistricting."
7 Ibid.
8 Iowa Code 2016, Section 42.4.5d. https://www.legis.iowa.gov/docs/code/2016/42.4.pdf (accessed July 7, 2020).
9 Ibid., Section 42.4.5.
10 Brennan Center for Justice. 2018. "Overview: Missouri Redistricting Reform Proposal (Clean Missouri)." October 12 https://www.brennancenter.org/our-work/policy-solutions/overview-missouri-redistricting-reform-proposal-clean-missouri (accessed July 8, 2020).
11 Ibid.

12 Ibid.
13 Vickrey, William. 1961. "On the Prevention of Gerrymandering." *Political Science Quarterly* 76: 110.
14 Nagel, Stuart S. 1965. "Simplified Bipartisan Computer Redistricting." *Stanford Law Review* 17: 863.
15 Altman, Micah. 1997. "The Computational Complexity of Automated Redistricting: Is Automation the Answer?" *Rutgers Computer & Technology Law Journal* 23: 81–142; Kueng, Richard, Dusting G. Mixon, and Soledad Villar. 2019. "Fair Redistricting is Hard." *Theoretical Computer Science* 791: 28–35.
16 Altman, "The Computational Complexity of Automated Redistricting," 101.
17 See, for example, Browdy, Michelle H. 1990. "Simulated Annealing: An Improved Computer Model for Political Redistricting." *Yale Law & Policy Review* 8: 169–72.
18 Altman, Micah and Michael McDonald. 2010. "The Promise and Perils of Computers in Redistricting." *Duke Journal of Constitutional Law & Public Policy* 5: 81.
19 Kueng, Mixon, and Villar, "Fair Redistricting is Hard," 29.
20 Altman, Micah and Michael McDonald. 2018. "Redistricting by Formula: An Ohio Reform Experiment." *American Politics Research* 46: 110. See also Altman and McDonald, "The Promise and Perils of Computers in Redistricting," 81–90.
21 Altman and McDonald, "The Promise and Perils of Computers in Redistricting," 91.
22 The use of a schema for distinguishing types of redistricting commissions based on levels of authority and independence is drawn from Edwards, Barry, Angel Sanchez, Tyler Yeargain, Michael Crespin, and Jessica Hayden. 2016. "Can Independent Redistricting Commissions Lead Us Out of the Political Thicket?" *Albany Government Law Review* 9: 288–340.
23 For details on redistricting commissions that draw congressional district lines, see National Conference of State Legislatures. 2019. "Redistricting Commissions: Congressional Plans." NCSL.org, April 18. https://www.ncsl.org/research/redistricting/redistricting-commissions-congressional-plans.aspx#Primary (accessed July 2, 2020).
24 National Conference of State Legislatures. 2019. "Redistricting Commissions: State Legislative Plans." NCSL.org, April 18. https://

www.ncsl.org/research/redistricting/2009-redistricting-commiss
ions-table.aspx#Commissions%20with%20Primary%20Responsi
bility (accessed January 7, 2020).

25 The details contained in the notes to table 6.1 are mostly taken from
National Conference of State Legislatures. 2020. "Redistricting
Commissions: State Legislative Plans." NCSL.org, January 9.
https://www.ncsl.org/research/redistricting/2009-redistricting-com
missions-table.aspx (accessed July 2, 2020).

26 Cain, Bruce E. 2012. "Redistricting Commissions: A Better Political
Buffer." *Yale Law Journal* 121: 1816.

27 Common Cause of Ohio. 2019. "Our New Redistricting Process in
Ohio." March 15. https://www.commoncause.org/ohio/resource/
our-new-redistricting-process-in-ohio/ (accessed July 2, 2020).

28 Campaign Legal Center. 2018. "Designing Independent
Redistricting Commissions." https://campaignlegal.org/sites/def
ault/files/2018-07/Designing_IRC_Report2_FINAL_Print.pdf,   9
(accessed July 3, 2020).

29 Ibid.

30 Rudensky, Yurij. 2018. "Arizona's Redistricting System is a Huge
Success. Some Legislators Want to Gut It." Brennan Center for
Justice. May 4. https://www.brennancenter.org/our-work/analysis-
opinion/arizonas-redistricting-system-huge-success-some-legislators-
want-gut-it

31 Ibid.

32 The steps that follow are as described by Common Cause of
California. N.d. "California Citizens Redistricting Commission,
Commissioner Selection Process." https://www.commoncause.org/
california/wp-content/uploads/sites/29/2018/05/CRC-Selection-
Graphic-FINAL-1.pdf (accessed July 3, 2020).

33 Ibid.

34 Brennan Center for Justice. 2018. "Overview: Proposed Colorado
Congressional Redistricting Reform Amendment (Amendment Y)."
October 12. https://www.brennancenter.org/our-work/research-
reports/overview-proposed-colorado-congressional-redistricting-
reform-amendment (accessed July 3, 2020).

35 Ibid.

36 See Colorado General Assembly. N.d. "Congressional
Redistricting." http://leg.colorado.gov/bills/scr18-004 (accessed
July 3, 2020); and Colorado General Assembly. N.d. "Legislative

Redistricting." http://leg.colorado.gov/bills/scr18-005 (accessed July 3, 2020).

37 Michigan Secretary of State. N.d. "Random Selection: Timeline." https://www.michigan.gov/sos/0,4670,7-127-1633_91141_100 903---,00.html (accessed July 3, 2020).

38 Brennan Center for Justice. 2018. "Overview: Michigan Redistricting Reform Proposal." August 17. https://www.brenn ancenter.org/our-work/research-reports/overview-michigan-redistr icting-reform-proposal (accessed July 3, 2020).

39 *Arizona State Legislature v. Arizona Independent Redistricting Commission* 576 U.S. ___ (2015).

40 See Green, Rebecca. 2018. "Redistricting Transparency." *William & Mary Law Review* 59: 1805–11.

41 Edwards, Barry, Michael Crespin, Ryan D. Williamson, and Maxwell Palmer. 2017. "Institutional Control of Redistricting and the Geography of Representation." *The Journal of Politics* 79: 722.

42 Ibid., 724–5.

43 Ibid., 725–6.

44 See Henderson, John A., Brian T. Hamel, and Aaron M. Goldzimer. 2018. "Gerrymandering Incumbency: Does Nonpartisan Redistricting Increase Electoral Competition?" *The Journal of Politics* 80: 1011–16; and Masket, Seth E., Jonathan Winburn, and Gerald C. Wright. 2012. "The Gerrymanderers Are Coming! Legislative Redistricting Won't Affect Competition or Polarization Much, No Matter Who Does It." *PS: Political Science & Politics* 45: 39–43.

45 See, for example, Carson, Jamie L. and Michael H. Crespin. 2004. "The Effect of State Redistricting Methods on Electoral Competition in United States House of Representatives Races." *State Politics & Policy Quarterly* 4: 455–69; Lindgren, Eric and Priscilla Southwell. 2013. "The Effect of Redistricting Commissions on Electoral Competitiveness in U.S. House Elections, 2002–2010." *Journal of Politics and Law* 6: 13–18; Goedert, Nicholas. 2017. "The Pseudoparadox of Partisan Mapmaking and Congressional Competition." *State Politics & Policy Quarterly* 17: 47–75; Williamson, Ryan D. 2019. "Examining the Effects of Partisan Redistricting on Candidate Entry Decisions." *Election Law Journal* 18: 214–26; and Seabrook, Nicholas R. 2017. *Drawing the Lines: Constraints on Partisan Gerrymandering in U.S. Politics*. Ithaca, NY: Cornell University Press, 108–16.

46 Carson, Jamie L., Michael H. Crespin, and Ryan D. Williamson. 2014. "Reevaluating the Effects of Redistricting on Electoral Competition, 1972–2012." *State Politics & Policy Quarterly* 14: 174.

47 Kang, Michael S. 2006. "De-Rigging Elections: Direct Democracy and the Future of Redistricting Reform." *Washington University Law Review* 84: 668.

48 Huefner, Steven F. 2010. "Don't Just Make Redistricters *More Accountable* to the People, Make *Them* the People." *Duke Journal of Constitutional Law & Public Policy* 5: 55.

49 Ibid., 63.

50 See McDonald, Michael and Micah Altman. 2018. *The Public Mapping Project: How Public Participation Can Revolutionize Redistricting*. Ithaca, NY: Cornell University Press.

51 Altman and McDonald, "Redistricting by Formula," 113–16.

52 Ibid., 114.

53 Ibid., 117.

54 Kang, "De-Rigging Elections," 704.

55 Ibid., 669.

56 Ibid.

57 Calabrese, Stephen. 2000. "Multimember District Congressional Elections." *Legislative Studies Quarterly* 25: 612.

58 National Conference of State Legislatures. 2018. "West Virginia Moves to Single-Member Districts." The NCSL Blog, April 10. https://www.ncsl.org/blog/2018/04/10/west-virginia-moves-to-single-member-districts.aspx (accessed July 8, 2020).

59 Ballotpedia. N.d. "State Legislative Chambers That Use Multi-member Districts." https://ballotpedia.org/State_legislative_cham bers_that_use_multi-member_districts (accessed July 8, 2020).

60 See, for instance, Engstrom, Richard and Michael McDonald. 1982. "The Underrepresentation of Blacks on City Councils: Comparing the Structural and Socioeconomic Explanations for South/Non-South Differences." *Journal of Politics* 44: 1088–99; Grofman, Bernard, Michael Migalski, and Nicholas Noviello. 1986. "Effects of Multimember Districts on Black Representation in State Legislatures." *Review of Black Political Economy* 14: 65–78; Bullock, Charles S. III and Ronald Keith Gaddie. 1993. "Changing from Multimember to Single-Member Districts: Partisan, Racial and Gender Consequences." *State and Local Government Review* 25:

155–63; Grofman, Bernard and Chandler Davidson. 1994. "The Effect of Municipal Election Structure on Black Representation in Eight Southern States." In *Quiet Revolution in the South*, eds. Chandler Davidson and Bernard Grofman. Princeton, NJ: Princeton University Press; and Gerber, Elizabeth R., Rebecca Morton, and Thomas A. Rietz. 1998. "Minority Representation in Multimember Districts." *American Political Science Review* 92: 127–44.

61 See Clark, Christopher J. 2019. *Gaining Voice: The Causes and Consequences of Black Representation in the American States*. New York: Oxford University Press, 41–5; and Herrnson, Paul S., Stella M. Rouse, and Jeffrey A. Taylor. 2020. "The Impact of Electoral Arrangements on Minority Representation: District Magnitude and the Election of African American State Legislators." *Election Law Journal* 19: 64–78.

62 Herrnson, Rouse, and Taylor, "The Impact of Electoral Arrangements on Minority Representation," 73.

63 Among many studies, see the classic account by Gudgin, Graham and Peter J. Taylor. 1979. *Seats, Votes, and the Spatial Organization of Elections*. London: Pion.

64 Zagarri, Rosemarie. 1987. *The Politics of Size: Representation in the United States, 1776–1850*. Ithaca, NY: Cornell University Press, 37.

65 Ibid.

66 Gardner, James A. 2007. "What is 'Fair' Partisan Representation, and How Can It Be Constitutionalized?: The Case for a Return to Fixed Election Districts." *Marquette Law Review* 90: 558.

67 Gallagher, Michael and Paul Mitchell. 2005. "Introduction to Electoral Systems." In *The Politics of Electoral Systems*, eds. Michael Gallagher and Paul Mitchell. New York: Oxford University Press, 3. See also Blais, André. 1988. "The Classification of Electoral Systems." *European Journal of Political Research* 16: 100.

68 Grofman, Bernard. 2008. "The Impact of Electoral Laws on Political Parties." In *The Oxford Handbook of Political Economy*, eds. Barry R. Weingast and Donald A. Wittman. New York: Oxford University Press, 104.

69 There are any number of excellent introductions to electoral systems around the world. See, for example, Farrell, David M. 2011. *Electoral Systems: A Comparative Introduction*, 2nd edn. London:

Red Globe Press. For a more detailed examination, see Herron, Erik S., Robert J. Pekkanen, and Matthew S. Shugart, eds. 2018. *The Oxford Handbook of Electoral Systems*. New York: Oxford University Press.

70 For the original demonstration of this conclusion, known as "Duverger's Law," see Duverger, Maurice. 1954. *Political Parties*. New York: John Wiley. There have been countless examinations of Duverger's Law since the original proposition.

71 For a review, see Eggers, Andrew C. and Alexander B. Fouirnaies. 2014. "Representation and District Magnitude in Plurality Systems." *Electoral Studies* 33: 267–77.

72 Ibid.

73 See Renwick, Alan. 2010. *The Politics of Electoral Reform: Changing the Rules of Democracy*. New York: Cambridge University Press.

74 See Shugart, Matthew Soberg and Martin P. Wattenberg. 2001. *Mixed-Member Electoral Systems: The Best of Both Worlds?* New York: Oxford University Press.

75 Cain, Bruce E. 2015. *Democracy More or Less: America's Political Reform Quandary*. New York: Cambridge University Press.

Bibliography

Ansolabehere, Stephen and James M. Snyder, Jr. 2008. *The End of Inequality: One Person, One Vote and the Transformation of American Politics*. New York: W.W. Norton & Company.

Balinski, Michel L. and H. Peyton Young. 2001. *Fair Representation: Meeting the Ideal of One Man, One Vote*, 2nd edn. Washington, DC: Brookings Institution Press.

Brunell, Thomas L. 2008. *Redistricting and Representation: Why Competitive Elections are Bad for America*. New York: Routledge.

Buchler, Justin. 2005. "Competition, Representation, and Redistricting: The Case against Competitive Congressional Districts." *Journal of Theoretical Politics* 17: 431–63.

Bullock, Charles S., III. 2010. *Redistricting: The Most Political Activity in America*. Lanham, MD: Rowman & Littlefield.

Butler, David and Bruce Cain. 1991. *Congressional Redistricting: Comparative and Theoretical Perspectives*. New York: Macmillan.

Cain, Bruce E. 2012. "Redistricting Commissions: A Better Political Buffer." *Yale Law Journal* 121: 1808–44.

Canon, David T. 1999. *Race, Redistricting, and Representation: The Unintended Consequences of Black Majority Districts*. Chicago, IL: University of Chicago Press.

Cox, Gary W. and Jonathan N. Katz. 2002. *Elbridge Gerry's Salamander: The Electoral Consequences of the Reapportionment Revolution*. New York: Cambridge University Press.

Daley, David. 2017. *Ratf**ked: The True Story Behind the Secret Plan to Steal America's Democracy*. New York: Liveright.

Duchin, Moon. 2018. "Geometry v. Gerrymandering." *Scientific American*, November: 49–53.

Durrance, Chris and Barak Goodman. 2020. *Slay the Dragon*. United States: Magnolia Pictures.

Edwards, Barry, Angel Sanchez, Tyler Yeargain, Michael Crespin, and

Jessica Hayden. 2016. "Can Independent Redistricting Commissions Lead Us out of the Political Thicket?" *Albany Government Law Review* 9: 288–340.

Engstrom, Erik J. 2016. *Partisan Gerrymandering and the Construction of American Democracy*. Ann Arbor, MI: University of Michigan Press.

Gelman, Andrew and Gary King. 1994. "Enhancing Democracy Through Legislative Redistricting." *American Political Science Review* 88: 541–59.

Griffith, Elmer C. 1907. *The Rise and Development of the Gerrymander*. Chicago, IL: Scott, Foresman, and Company.

Grofman, Bernard and Lisa Handley, eds. 2008. *Redistricting in Comparative Perspective*. New York: Oxford University Press.

Gudgin, Graham and Peter J. Taylor. 1979. *Seats, Votes, and the Spatial Organization of Elections*. London: Pion.

Lublin, David. 1997. *The Paradox of Representation: Racial Gerrymandering and Minority Interests in Congress*. Princeton, NJ: Princeton University Press.

McDonald, Michael P. and Micah Altman. 2018. *The Public Mapping Project: How Public Participation Can Revolutionize Redistricting*. Ithaca, NY: Cornell University Press.

McGann, Anthony, Charles Anthony Smith, Michael Latner, and Alex Keena. 2016. *Gerrymandering in America: The House of Representatives, the Supreme Court, and the Future of Popular Sovereignty*. New York: Cambridge University Press.

Monmonier, Mark. 2001. *Bushmanders & Bullwinkles: How Politicians Manipulate Electronic Maps and Census Data to Win Elections*. Chicago, IL: University of Chicago Press.

Rush, Mark E. 1993. *Does Redistricting Make a Difference? Partisan Representation and Electoral Behavior*. Baltimore, MD: Johns Hopkins University Press.

Seabrook, Nicholas R. 2017. *Drawing the Lines: Constraints on Partisan Gerrymandering in U.S. Politics*. Ithaca, NY: Cornell University Press.

Smith, J. Douglas. 2014. *On Democracy's Doorstep: The Inside Story of How the Supreme Court Brought 'One Person, One Vote' to the United States*. New York: Hill and Wang.

Squire, Peverill. 2012. *The Evolution of American Legislatures: Colonies, Territories, and States, 1619–2009*. Ann Arbor, MI: University of Michigan Press.

Winburn, Jonathan. 2008. *The Realities of Redistricting: Following the Rules and Limiting Gerrymandering in State Legislative Redistricting.* Lanham, MD: Lexington Books.

Yoshinaka, Antoine and Chad Murphy. 2011. "The Paradox of Redistricting: How Partisan Mapmakers Forster Competition but Disrupt Representation." *Political Research Quarterly* 64: 435–47.

Zagarri, Rosemarie. 1987. *The Politics of Size: Representation in the United States, 1776–1850.* Ithaca, NY: Cornell University Press.

Index

Abramowitz, Alan 107, 112–13, 115, 136, 137
accountability
  and dyadic representation 18
  elected officials and redistricting 15
  redistricting commissions 155
aggressive gerrymanders 117
Alabama
  Tuskegee district boundaries 59–60
Alaska
  redistricting commission 148, 150
Alexander, Brad 107
Alexander, Larry 11–12
Altman, Micah 87–9, 90–1, 133, 147, 156
Ansolabehere, Stephen 48–9, 51, 55, 124
Apportionment Act (1842) 43–4
Arbour, Brian 117
Arizona 79, 148
Arkansas 22, 78
  independent citizen redistricting commissions 148, 149, 151, 153

Basehart, Harry 125
bias 5, 91–101
  and the consequences of gerrymandering 106
  district maps 59, 91–2

intentionally biased maps 92–101
and multimember districts 160
partisan advantage 45, 111–23
see also partisan gerrymandering
bicameral assemblies 29
the "big sort" 93–4
bipartisan gerrymandering
  (incumbent protection) 5, 45
and the civic redistricting perspective 23–4
and competition 108, 109, 110–11
drawing district maps 84, 95–6, 102
impact of 105, 123–8, 130, 138
marginal incumbents 123
"out-party" incumbents 126
and partisan gerrymandering 84–5
and polarization 135
and the realpolitik argument 9–10
and representation 23
voters in new districts 127, 130, 138
bipartisan maps 45
Bishop, Bill 93
bizarreness of districts 81, 82
black voters
  impact of redistricting on 129
  see also racial gerrymandering
Born, Richard 127, 131